REVOLUTIONARY WAR
GHOSTS
OF CONNECTICUT

COURTNEY McINVALE

HAUNTED
AMERICA

Published by Haunted America
A Division of The History Press
Charleston, SC
www.historypress.net

Cover photo by author.

First published 2016

Manufactured in the United States

ISBN 978.1.46711.880.4

Library of Congress Control Number: 2016934638

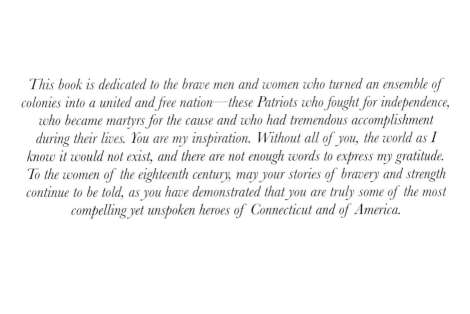

This book is dedicated to the brave men and women who turned an ensemble of colonies into a united and free nation—these Patriots who fought for independence, who became martyrs for the cause and who had tremendous accomplishment during their lives. You are my inspiration. Without all of you, the world as I know it would not exist, and there are not enough words to express my gratitude. To the women of the eighteenth century, may your stories of bravery and strength continue to be told, as you have demonstrated that you are truly some of the most compelling yet unspoken heroes of Connecticut and of America.

CONTENTS

ACKNOWLEDGEMENTS

To write about the history and haunts surrounding a pivotal colony during the forging of nation is far too large an undertaking for one author, and this book could not have been completed without hours of talks, tours and discussions with historians, spiritual mediums, homestead interpreters, archivists and more. Each person contributed unique and unrivaled knowledge to this book, and I want to extend wholehearted thanks to each and every one of you who shared your knowledge and your locations with me.

To Jennifer Emerson: the titles of author, consultant, actress, historian and spiritualist don't begin to cover the extent of your ability and knowledge. Your passion for historical material, your connection with Lucretia Shaw and your ability to immerse yourself in the authenticity of eighteenth-century society in order to paint a beautiful picture transported me back in time and allowed me to feel as if I truly walked among the most powerful women and men of the 1770s. You shine a beautiful light, and I am in awe of your knowledge and dedication to those who walked Connecticut centuries ago.

To Robert Lecce: whether it's through your work as a guide, a colonial reenactor, a budding spirit sensitive or historical researcher, you breathe new life into the tours, the investigations and everything you put your heart and soul into. Your willingness to don your Revolutionary-era best and exchange in conversation with spirits of the past, educate locals of the amazing history that surrounds them and participate in paranormal investigations gave enormous contribution and motivation to this book. Your enthusiasm and respect for the living and the dead is unrivaled. This book, these investigations and Seaside Shadows could not exist without you.

To Stacey Phillips and Austin Mann: the sharing of your spiritual gifts and your loyalty mean the world to a para-historian like myself. You have the ability to sense the importance of historic figures and commensurate spirit activity by just stepping into a building. You possess true dedication to the spiritual and historical missions we embark on together. Thank you for joining me in the dead of night at places across the state to learn of all things history and ghosts together.

To Bill Lee, town historian emeritus of Fairfield, artist and true "renaissance man": our conversations where you imparted your detailed knowledge of the Sun Tavern to me, alongside your personal experiences of life within the Sun Tavern alongside your beautiful wife, Anne, will live forever in my memory. I can only hope to have given enough credit to you for your salvation of the Sun Tavern and in allowing me to tell both yours and the tavern's colorful story.

To the Connecticut Sons of the American Revolution Chapter, former president Stephen Shaw and property steward Dave Packard: your contributions were numerous. Stephen, your knowledge of the Lebanon War Office is something that could not be found anywhere else—you truly knew more of that building's history than is available in any book. Dave, you drove me all over the state to each location, talked to me of history, met at each place late at night for investigations and believed in me and this book from our very first conversation.

To Lou Sorrentino: what can I say except thank you for following your heart, for dedicating your life to others, for your empathetic nature and for finding the millstone at Chapman Falls in Devil's Hopyard. From the moment you uncovered the millstone, your quest for knowledge about Abner Beebe and the Sons of Liberty was unending. I cannot wait to see the exhibit in the Smithsonian in 2017—all because of your dedication to a previously untold story. Thank you for sharing with me your research and passion.

A special thanks to the following people whose contributions were essential and crucial to the completion of this book: Stephen Marshall; Nathan Hale Homestead, as well as Ted Jarrett, Linda Pagliuco, Matthew Flegert; New London Country Historical Society, as well as Kayla Correll, Steve Manuel, Marilyn Davis; Society of the Founders of Norwich, Leffingwell House Museum, as well as Greg and Cam Farlow and Richard Guidebeck; Connecticut Department of Environmental and Energy Protection, as well as Eric Gileau; Fairfield Museum and History Center, as well as Georgiana

Platt; Hempsted Houses, as well as Barbara Nagy; Connecticut Landmarks; Paranormal Research Society of New England, as well as John Zaffis, Carlos Reis, Dominick Onofrio, Dan LeRoy; Evan Andriopoulos; New London Landmarks, as well as Constance Kristofik; Brent Colley and Shamus Denniston; New England Spiritual Team Inc., as well as Michael Carroll; Elisabeth Angel Pfeifer; Ghosts of New England Research Society, Kurt Knapp; DKS Paranormal; CCSU's Society of Paranormal Research, as well as Brian Field and Tom Keane; Shelby McInvale and Jeff Fillback; Tom D'Agostino; Pine Grove Spiritualist Camp; Niantic Book Barn, as well as Randy White; and author Eric Lehman. There are not enough words to express my gratitude to each and every one of you.

Last but certainly not least, I thank my family and friends for their unwavering support during the completion of this book.

My thanks go out to everyone I met along this incredible journey. Without you, *Revolutionary War Ghosts of Connecticut* would not be in print, and the amazing history and ghosts of the Nutmeg State would not be able to transport readers back in time to Connecticut's rebellious roots.

INTRODUCTION

The phrase "the Patriots" is one we use frequently here in New England, but in the twenty-first century, it is rarely used within the same regional context it was in the late 1700s. It is not usually in reference to men such as infamous spy Nathan Hale, General George Washington, Samuel Adams (the man and the legacy that influenced the iconic Boston brew), John Hancock (more than just a signature) or any of the Sons of Liberty. Instead, we refer to the American football team the New England Patriots, a household name for many. Rarely do we stop and think about the name "Patriot" as being iconic to the region, as it represented the earliest thoughts and ideas that bred a nation.

Connecticut, officially known as the Constitution State, has always been at the forefront of eighteenth-century history on this side of the pond known as the Atlantic. Revolutionary names and legacies have become so ingrained into the founding of nearly everything New England has created—so common that its origins innocently pass our minds. However, the origins of the name "Patriot" as we know it, the world in which these men and women Patriots and their opposition lived, the manner in which they conducted themselves, the war they fought and the legacy every single one of them left behind are palpable throughout early colonies. Connecticut played a pivotal role in the stories of Revolutionaries and Loyalists alike. These lives and their legacies live on in historic sites and artifacts that exist throughout the Constitution State today.

Ask many paranormal investigators what their goal is in looking into a "haunted location" and they will tell you that they long to learn from

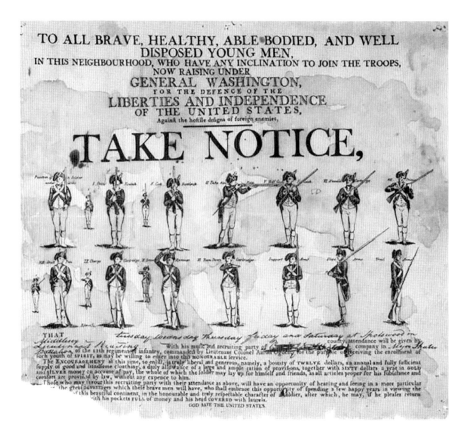

Revolutionary War Continental army recruitment poster, circa 1775. *Courtesy of the Society of the Founders of Norwich and Leffingwell House Museum.*

someone who came before them. Is it possible that we can learn from the very men and women responsible for the forging of a nation as we know it today through contact with their spirits? Are these spirits at historic sites that they either lived in, frequented or had attachment to? Many visitors, historical interpreters, investigators and more would suggest that indeed they are still there and perhaps that they still have history to teach us.

Many of these Connecticut locations saw men and women who changed the face of America. Travel throughout Connecticut and look into mirrors that General George Washington gazed into during his travels, walk through taverns that Benedict Arnold and the Sons of Liberty frequented, stroll through the halls where John Hancock married his bride (the very same building where Sam Adams was a Revolutionary refugee in a Loyalist region), stand where men lost their lives at the last remaining complete Revolutionary war site and battlefield and walk through the woods where Tory men were exposed and made vulnerable for standing by their king. Meeting rooms, mansions, mill houses and more abound—buildings that stood here when the nation as we know it was forged and witnessed the masterminds behind it. All this lies within the Nutmeg State. In Connecticut, the Revolutionary history and haunts penetrate the land, the vibration sits in the air and the spirits still walk with stories to tell. Travel with the ghosts of the Continental army throughout Connecticut's rebellious haunts.

Nathan Hale's Connecticut Stomping Grounds

Tales from the Homestead in Coventry, East Haddam Schoolhouse and New London Schoolhouse

Nathan Hale is often referred to as the first true American hero, the earliest spy of the Patriot cause and a man of great accomplishment in a brief twenty-one years on earth. The truth is that he was all of those things—not merely a man of myth or legend. Admittedly, it's difficult for most to fathom that a man, one of twelve siblings raised in small-town eighteenth-century Connecticut by a deacon, could become a stunning athlete, a true academic, a Yale graduate, a teacher who broke the rules and even schooled young women before it was tradition, a soldier and a spy commissioned by George Washington—all in one lifetime. In twenty-one years, Nathan Hale accomplished all of these feats and did Coventry and the state of Connecticut more than proud. Nathan's legacy is perhaps best immortalized by his final words, as documented by British officers at the time of his capture and hanging: "I only regret that I have but one life to lose for my country."

Although some controversy has been met over whether he truly spoke those words, it's widely acknowledged that Hale was a fan and student of Joseph Addison's *Cato* during his studies at Yale, and that is where Hale first became familiar with that quotation. Thus it stands to reason that this very sentiment was likely a true motivator for him. Also, British officers such as Captain William Montresor and Lieutenant Robert MacKensie, who documented his final words, would have no reason to fabricate a saying like this coming from the mouth of Hale. They documented it as a fact, even though they would have had to acknowledge that it would be considered a heroic statement by their opposition.

Fascinatingly enough, Nathan Hale's legacy wouldn't truly develop throughout Connecticut and the country until more than a decade after his execution. The Hale family name became recognized, the schoolhouses he taught in were memorialized and the homestead his family built was revived in the early twentieth century. All of this dedication to his cause and name would not be seen until more than a century later, with all of these museums in his name.

Nathan himself wasn't the only true hero of the family, but to be a brand-new nation's martyr is an immense legacy and story to tell. Nathan was born on June 6, 1755, in Coventry, Connecticut, and was a sickly infant. His mother and family devoted extra time and nurturing to young Nathan as he began to grow into a healthy, sturdy young boy, and his days of frailty were soon a memory of distant past. The Nathan Hale Homestead, built in 1776, sits in the exact spot where the smaller house Nathan was actually born in once stood. In fact, bits of the foundation woodwork of the former home were utilized in the building of the new home, and the old kitchen was kept as an addition to the new home, including a great part of the former home at that time. The now-old kitchen is considered to be the most dated part of the house and possibly the only part that Nathan would have stepped foot in during his life in Coventry. Construction on the current homestead was not completed until the year of his death, and most of it took place while he was serving in the Revolutionary War. Army records do not indicate vacations or breaks for Nathan during this time. However, some believe that when Nathan was in the area, he stopped back in Coventry to assist in the building of the family homestead.

Nathan's parents were Deacon Richard Hale and Elizabeth Strong. Nathan Hale was, in fact, a great-grandson of Reverend John Hale from Beverly, Massachusetts, a judge during the famous Salem Witch Trials alongside Samuel Parris. Nathan's great-grandfather had indeed assisted in the prosecution of witches but later withdrew when accusations were pointed at his own family member. The Hale family's contribution to the prosecution of innocents was then officially renounced. Nevertheless, this little-known Salem Witch Trial legacy was rarely spoken about by the Hale family in Coventry—and rightfully so, as they changed the legacy of what the Hale family name would come to mean throughout New England.

Sketch of Nathan Hale Homestead in Coventry, circa 1800s. *Courtesy of Yale University Library.*

Nathan was the sixth of twelve children, one of nine boys in the Hale family—six of whom would go on to fight in the Revolutionary War in some regard. He was considered to be a charmer and was described as both attractive and well-built and muscular. He had great athletic talent in football (which he played at Yale) and had distinct blue eyes and light reddish to brown hair. What's interesting is that an official portrait was never completed of young Nathan, and only descriptions from journals and portraits of his siblings allow any of us a glimpse as to what he may have looked like. Statues, portraits and more were created over the centuries, immortalizing an idea of his appearance; none of them was made knowing of his likeness, and they are instead artistic renderings. The closest we can get to knowing at least his facial shape is an etching that the Hale family had done of his silhouette on a door after his passing. This door was actually removed from the house years later and salvaged by George Dudley Seymour, who turned the Nathan Hale house into the museum it became, recovered family artifacts, wrote a book of Hale's life and dedicated his life to the importance of the Coventry site. Once he found it, Seymour actually stole the door alongside an acquaintance and carried it on his back to have the etching uncovered by an expert. When this was done and it was confirmed to show the silhouette of young Nathan, it was said to be the moment Seymour decided to buy the property and resurrect it from the shambles it had been in. The etching can be seen on the door to this very day when touring the museum.

Portrait of Nathan Hale, circa 1960 and 1970s. *Courtesy of the Connecticut Sons of the American Revolution.*

Besides good looks and athleticism, Nathan's aptitude for learning was clear, and he was enrolled in Yale by his father when he was just fourteen years old alongside his brother Enoch, who was then sixteen years old. A charming, handsome, intelligent young man, he graduated at the age of eighteen in 1773 alongside thirty-six other men. One of his most notable classmates was Benjamin Tallmadge, an officer in the Continental army under Washington who went on to lead the Culper spy ring, for which he is popularly known. Tallmadge and Hale, who had become fast and best friends, were also participants in one of the biggest debates of academia at the time: the education of young women (of which they were in favor). However, it is well-documented that it was under Tallmadge's influence and correspondence that young Nathan joined up for the cause himself.

But not quite yet. After Nathan and Benjamin's graduation, Tallmadge went on to received employment in Wethersfield as a superintendent in education. As for Hale, his ambition was to teach, and he received his first job offer in East Haddam, Connecticut, a town of country people and farms—not exactly what an ambitious young man was hoping for in regards to environment, yet it was a teaching position where an impact could be made molding young minds. So, Hale took the position and taught in East Haddam for about six months before accepting a job offer in the big city of New London, where he would stay as an instructor for just over a year before his enrollment in the Continental army's Seventh Connecticut Regiment. The East Haddam Schoolhouse, where Hale taught, remains to the present day, having been moved twice—first located close to the river, then to a nearby church up a road and subsequently, and finally, to its location now in the hillside above the church overlooking the glorious Connecticut River and the environment it has always served. The East Haddam and New London Schoolhouses are owned and operated by the Connecticut Sons of the American Revolution. They are active museums in the community, both named after Nathan Hale, and can be visited today; they filled with information on Hale and the schoolhouse past.

As for Hale, he documented immense boredom in East Haddam and was eagerly applying to other towns while he worked there. A young man, he desired a city, which he can't be blamed for, but for six months he was a schoolmaster for the young men in central Connecticut of varying ages. It's unknown whether Hale began his unprecedented education of young women while in East Haddam or if that came into play later, when he was in New London, but it is indeed possible that he was the inaugural schoolmaster to teach girls of East Haddam. East Haddam schooling hours would've been different than in the city. The children were often expected to work on the surrounding family farms first thing in the morning and in the early evening—leaving only midday for lessons or just after morning chores. Farm life and education had to work in tandem with each other

Nathan Hale Schoolhouse in East Haddam, circa 1940. *Courtesy of the Library of Congress.*

for parents to support the local education, and the parents had to pay for everything their child utilized and even a portion of the heating costs for the school. If parents could not afford that, a child in the eighteenth century was not required to go to school and thus usually didn't. Later on, of course, in encouraging education, parents would be fined for not sending their child to school.

Nevertheless, after a brief semester in East Haddam, Hale moved to bigger and (to him, at least) better things in the big city of New London, where he could have a social life, court the ladies, participate in rebel discussion and educate at a much larger schoolhouse. He became the preceptor of Union School, a school funded by trustees Nathaniel and Lucretia Shaw, to whom he would become of great acquaintance. The school is known today as the Nathan Hale Schoolhouse of New London and is known to have been a place of education of young women by Mr. Hale. He would have educated them sometimes early in the morning before the arrival of the boys but usually on Saturdays, believing in their abilities and equal right to education. Many who did not believe that this was right attacked Hale's integrity and character for this, but Nathan remained unwavering and steadfast in his belief. Caulkin's *History of New London* describes the young schoolmaster as viewed by his acquaintance and comrades in New London: "Frank and independent in his bearing, social, animated, ardent, a lover of the society of ladies, and a favorite among them."

Unquestionably, although he was young, Hale was an honest and upstanding gentleman. Hale educated daily the likes of thirty-two young boys, and the lengthwise tables on which they sat holding their slates can be seen in the schoolhouse today—multiple boys on benches, scraping what they could on slates to commit information to memory because paper was a commodity hard to come by and quite an undertaking to make. They were primarily educated in Latin and grammar. The Union School was one of the few buildings that went on to survive the Burning of New London in 1781 and thus remains as a memory of Nathan Hale's legacy within the southeastern Connecticut city.

During their careers in education, both Tallmadge and Hale were surrounded by those who participated in "radical" politics of the time with their new teaching—Tallmadge by Silas Deane and Hale by the Shaws and the Hempsteads, who came to see Hale as an idol and later served under him in the Seventh Connecticut Regiment. Hale was a committed schoolteacher but soon seemed to reach boredom once more, even in the great city of

Postcard of Nathan Hale Schoolhouse in New London, circa 1909. *Courtesy of the Connecticut Sons of the American Revolution.*

New London, and had a deep desire to do more. This desire and ambition, following written exchanges with Tallmadge, ultimately inspired Hale to join the New London militia, where in less than a year, by the summer of 1775, he was promoted to first sergeant. Hale and Tallmadge continued correspondence, and just two weeks after Washington came through Connecticut in 1775, Hale resigned from the New London school and joined the Seventh Connecticut Regiment.

Hale accompanied his regiment to the Siege of Boston, where he livened up the camp with activities and sports, keeping up the mood of his men. He took his duty seriously, as documented in his journals, but wanted to keep his fellow men's spirits up. As Hale began service, his personality was sorely missed in New London by friends and ladies, as letters show. Hale, however, had made his commitment at that time to forging a new country. He was promoted to captain within the regiment and became a leader and symbol of integrity to many. Throughout his service, he continued in correspondence of updates and good jest to both Tallmadge and his brothers, who were serving elsewhere or happened to be at home in Coventry.

It was September 1, 1776, when Hale's mission as a spy officially began. Washington administered a request for intelligence to all of his generals, and the request eventually reached the ears of Nathan Hale, who was eager to make a difference after not having served in battle and saw this as his opportunity to make a statement and a difference. One of Hale's close friends from Yale who was stationed nearby was uncomfortable with Hale's becoming a confidential informant and spy. He didn't think that Hale had the personality for it, and to be fair, with a reputation like Hale's, people worried about him. A spy on either side of the war was often seen, even by their own men, as a traitor—if they could make a business out of lying, who was to say if they could be acting as a double agent or if they were truly honest men. Spies were seen very differently at the time compared to today.

Hale pushed this all aside and agreed to fulfill the general's request and gather intelligence. He took off to New York for a time with Hempstead at his side, before having him return home to Hale's family with his belongings, including his notable shoe buckles. Hale was to assume the role of a Dutch schoolmaster, and he took with him his Yale diploma and humble attire so as not to raise suspicion. Controversy remains to this day about how Nathan Hale was caught in the weeks following, and his career as a spy indeed lasted only three weeks long. Some believe that his cousin, a Loyalist, followed Hale and turned him in, although he would later deny it. Others believe that a beautiful woman could have gotten the truth out of him as he had drinks at a local tavern. Most believe that Hale was found out through another man claiming to be a spy—a man of the Tories who, after a few drinks, said to Hale, "I'm a spy as well. We should work together," or something of that sort. Hale, a young man full of trust and his senses diminished from alcohol, agreed and let the man know that he was a spy.

However it happened, General Howe of the Loyalists ordered Hale's execution. He was captured in Manhattan and hanged in front of all citizens on September 22, 1776. As he stood on the gallows platform, contemplating his brief life lived and bidding farewell to a future he would never see, he uttered those famous words: "I only regret that I have but one life to lose for my country." The provost marshal yelled the orders, "Swing the rebel off," and the noose was lifted, Hale's neck inside. He was killed right then and there in front of righteous Tories, frightened Patriots and confused city folk. Hale was left hanging there for three days as a sign to all of what being a traitor to England would mean before he was cut down and buried underneath the tree from which he was hanged. Various sites in New York boast to be the spot of Nathan Hale's burial, although no one knows for sure. Most believe that he lies somewhere under what is now Wall Street in Manhattan. His brother requested to bring his body home and did arrive days later but was denied his request. The Nathan Hale grave marker in Coventry, Connecticut, among his family is a memorial put there by his father, although his body never was brought home.

American knowledge of Hale's words and service did not come until later and were really made public after the execution and exhumation of Major John Andre, one of the most notable intelligence officers of the Loyalist side. Andre is known for many things but especially his occupation of Ben Franklin's house, as well as for his responsibility in turning Benedict Arnold and working alongside him at the attempted surrender of the fort at West Point. Andre was counterpart to many British intelligence missions and hence was executed upon capture by the Americans in 1780, four years after Hale's execution at the hands of Andre's allies. Much like Hale, Andre had an upstanding reputation as a man of both charm and integrity whom men on both sides of the war claimed to like. But when Andre was captured, it was time for retribution and retaliation for what had been done to Hale. When Tallmadge accompanied prisoner Andre on a trip to see Washington, Andre inquired of Tallmadge if he would be treated and regarded as a British officer or as a prisoner. Tallmadge, best friend of Hale, had an interesting response. He told Andre the entire story of Nathan Hale at

Depiction of Nathan Hale's hanging in New York on September 22, 1776. Painting by Albert Herter, circa 1913. *Courtesy of the Library of Congress.*

Yale—as educator, as soldier and as spy—and then followed with a question posed to Andre: "Do you remember the sequel to this story?"

Andre assented that he did and informed Tallmadge he knew he was hanged as a spy. Tallmadge looked Andre directly in the eye, not moved by his charm or reputation, and replied, "And similar will be your fate."

After trial, Andre was executed by hanging on October 2, 1780, in New York near West Point and buried again at the gallows where he met his fate. To the horror of Americans, the British came back in 1821 and had Andre's body exhumed and reburied in Westminster Abbey with full honors. Outrage ensued at this, and it was around this time that it became known and widely acknowledged that Andre's death was, in part, in direct retaliation for Hale's. The vengeful public agreed that this was right, and Hale's name began its heroic journey throughout the country. Nathan's legacy and story are told at both schoolhouses and his homestead in Coventry by all the interpreters, guides and museum donors you'll meet. Nathan made the ultimate sacrifice and for this became the hero of Connecticut and of a new nation.

The story of his other family members and their descendants' legacies should not remain untold, and if you visit the Nathan Hale Homestead, they will tell you of the greatness of their lives, as well as the life of George Dudley Seymour, who brought Nathan Hale's detailed story to life and also left a bit of his spirit within the home's walls, a place he loved dearly. Perhaps most notable of Nathan's brothers for their service are John and Joseph. Lieutenant Joseph Hale served in the Revolution and ended up a captured prisoner kept on a British ship off the coast of New Jersey, chained to the hull and deprived of decency, sustenance and hygiene. During this time, he contracted consumption and returned to the Hale Homestead to be among family. He brought with him his wife and daughters. Due to his declining health, he couldn't farm any longer. For three years, he held strong but passed away in 1784, surrounded by his loved ones. He was the tender age of thirty-four when he died within the house from the terrible, ravaging disease.

Seymour swore that he believed that Joseph's spirit made itself known by the cellar stairs, where the sounds of chains banging against the wall and accompanying wailing moans would be frequently heard—chains that only Joseph would've been acquainted with, like the chains that bound him as a prisoner of war. Guides over the years have also heard the mysterious clanking of chains by the same stairway area and can't help but wonder if it is indeed Joseph. Consumption moved through the Hale family, both extended and immediate, once Joseph brought it to the homestead. It was highly contagious, and some had no immunity to it—including brother Billie, who passed away from the contracted disease in 1785 at only twenty-six years old. Brother John Hale may have been considered one of the lucky ones, as he did not contract consumption or die during service.

It was ultimately John Hale who inherited the property from his father, Deacon Richard Hale. John had served after the Battle at Lexington, where he rose to the rank of major. When discharged, John came back to the homestead in Coventry, where he and his father were joint commission heads in charge of raising food for the troops and their families. Other than his time in service, John spent his entire life on that property from birth to death and raised his children there as well. At one time, there were as many as twenty-five Hales documented as living at the property. Although it may seem like a mansion for its time, its rooms were filled with family. Eldest brother Samuel Hale had also served in the war, but upon his return to the family homestead he seemed distant, introverted and unable to interact with many. He lived in a small building on the corner of the property suffering from what would seem to us today to be PTSD until his death as older man of seventy-seven in 1824. The effects of the war led Samuel to lead a life of solitude, and in his own way, he also gave life to his country. One odd result of this is that at one time a caretaker committed suicide not far from where Samuel had lived. Residual haunting or a breeding of energy in one spot may have resulted, some may say, but sadness simply struck the Hale family. The Hales had a great commitment to service, and Coventry was a heavily patriotic area of the state to which they equaled in feeling with unequivocal measure.

Some believe that the most frequently heard and seen spirits are that of John Hale and his wife, Sarah, the ones who inherited the property and spent a lifetime there. Within the homestead, there is a room that would have been John's parlor—decorated as vintage early American, a little less Revolutionary in décor and more New Republic than the room adjacent across the hall, which was Deacon Richard Hale's parlor. It is family patriarch Deacon Richard Hale that George Dudley Seymour and numerous historic interpreters believe may be the most prominent ghostly presence at the homestead. Having dedicated his life to his family, to service and to the building of that home, it seems quite fitting that it would remain his homestead today.

One of the most memorable ghostly encounters came from George Dudley Seymour's documentation in the early 1900s. Seymour was a man of many friends, some in high places, and he loved to entertain and host parties. He would dress in his best and show off his home with pride. His guests would take a train and then a horse and wagon to the old homestead in Coventry at the turn of the twentieth century. One evening, as Seymour was preparing for the festivities to begin, his guests began to arrive at the house; one of his friends from the New Haven area, taken with the beautiful property, ran up to the window to peer inside. As he ran to the window, he was greeted by another face, but it was not the face of his friend George. It was the face of a man who appeared older, was clad in colonial clothes, wore a tricorn hat and then vanished into thin air. His friends were taken so aback by this ghostly visage that they took off and refused to step foot into the house. Seymour later documented that he and his friend believed it was

Nathan Hale Homestead street view in Coventry, circa 2015.

a version of Deacon Richard Hale whom they saw peering back at them through the window.

Richard Hale seems to keep quite the eye on house visitors, especially young children who may not be paying close enough attention to the historic tour. Historic interpreter Matthew Flegert shared another guide's tale of a child's encounter with a Hale gentleman. A boy and his parents came for a tour; the boy, only about six or seven, had no interest in history and was running around the house away from the group and into varying rooms. Suddenly, the boy ran back to his parents, quiet as a mouse and clinging to his mom's arm with a strange look on his face. After moments of clinging in silence, the mother inquired, "What's wrong?" The boy responded, "The man pointed and yelled at me." "What are you talking about?" the mother responded with nervous laughter. The boy looked around to show the man to his parents, saw the picture of Nathan's brother John Hale and said, "It's that man; that's the man that yelled at me." No one knew what to make of it. The young boy had no idea who the man in the portrait was, but it seemed that John thought he should. John Hale only had one child, who passed away in infancy, and would not have been used to a rambunctious child running around the house. Other children have run around the homestead and also reported sightings of men in period attire to their parents and guides over the years. A child's sensitivity often opens up activity within any haunted location, be it a home, a museum or a combination of both.

The stories of haunts at the Nathan Hale Homestead range in such number that there are entire tours dedicated to the ghostly occurrences of the place, given every October by the team of guides, each with his or her own stories to tell. The homestead is now run by Connecticut Landmarks director Ted Jarrett, and historic interpreters do a phenomenal job of educating the public about all things Hale at the Coventry homestead. Upon request, they will inform you of all things ghostly.

Interpreters Matthew Flegert and Linda Pagliuco each had a spine-tingling experience to relate. Linda spoke of a time with her friend Leslie. It was 2003, and Linda, Leslie and others were members of the local Cemetery Commission, which had its monthly meetings at the homestead. It was late winter, with a little snow left on the ground and a rather early sunset on the evening of this meeting. Linda asserted, "The house is a whole different place at night, and no one really wants to be there alone." Linda and Leslie agreed that they would open up the museum together for the meeting around 7:00 p.m. Linda arrived a few moments early and parked in the drive, awaiting her friend's arrival. Less than ten minutes later, she saw the headlights of her friend Leslie's vehicle encroach slowly up the drive—a little too slowly. Linda was concerned. Was she having car troubles? Leslie parked with no car troubles at all. She had been driving slowly after she saw something strange in the window: the light was on. She was surprised to see that Linda had gone in on her own. Leslie was taken more aback when she stepped out of her car and Linda stepped out of her car to greet her. Leslie said, "Oh, I thought you were in the house. I saw the kitchen light on. Is someone else in the house?" Linda replied, "No, I don't think so." "Well, that's weird," Leslie replied hesitantly.

Together they decided to go into the house and joked with each other to lighten the mood. They went inside, turned the light off and set up for their meeting, where they just had to share their story. Others joked with the ladies and determined that Leslie's headlights likely reflected off the snow and gave the impression of the light being on. Leslie and Linda felt differently. They stayed until the end of the meeting and then locked up the house and shut off all the lights. Leslie asked if Linda would wait for her for a few moments. She wanted to approach the house the way she came in with her car and see if she could re-create the light and confirm that it was snow in order to debunk what she had seen. Linda watched as Leslie drove to South Street and then back up the driveway a few times. She said that she could not re-create the image that a light was on inside. It was dark and clearly not what she had seen the first time. It couldn't have been anything else. Matthew Flegert supports the claim and explained that numerous people have seen mysterious light anomalies in the windows.

Matthew's most memorable ghostly occurrence was in the summer of 2014 in the early evening. There was still plenty of light outside, and he was casually sitting within the attached gift shop reading Seymour's biography of Nathan Hale—doing a little job research, you could say. Another guide was in the house not far from him, and they had been preparing to close up soon. There is a main door by the store, and another one that enters in by the kitchen is normally only utilized by staff as it's a solid, heavy, unmoving door. As Matthew sat there reading, he heard the door open and footsteps enter the house. He didn't look up immediately, thinking that it was the director of the homestead coming in. He continued to hear the footsteps walk through the

Nathan Hale Homestead in Coventry, circa 2015. *Photo by Martin J. Reardon Jr.*

hall, figuring it to be the other guide near to him. Matthew thought, "Well, that's strange," as the director would normally greet them. So Matthew, thinking that it might be a rogue visitor, walked through the house, checked all the floors and found no one there. He went back to the store, having shut the door, and went back to his book. Suddenly, a terrible, annoying sound went off all around him—it was the security system indicating that someone had been inside. Matt and the other guide tried to figure it out. The other guide ensured that no one was in the house, while Matt shut the alarms off. Thinking it was such a strange day, Matt went back once more to his reading. If footsteps happened again, he wasn't going to get up again. This was crazy. Sure enough, as he sat back down the footsteps began walking through the house. He didn't see anyone else. That was it—his arms were covered in goose bumps, and he knew that someone else was there, a guest or a resident of the ghostly kind. It was friendly it seemed, not frightening, but clearly it was making itself known.

It's not just footsteps or lights that the guides may experience—sometimes it's actual verbal communication. Linda Pagliuco's most frightening encounter was around 2012. Linda wasn't expecting anything strange, having worked at the property since the '80s. She always felt safe there—so safe that she was the only guide who would let someone go home at closing if they needed to while she stayed to take around any late-arriving guests. Although the home is usually open only until four o'clock, guides will take guests who arrive fifteen minutes before closing. On this particular fall day, that's exactly what happened. The other guide went home, and Linda stayed to take the family around. The tour takes about forty-five minutes to an hour, and all went smoothly for that hour. As she had begun the tour, she saw the other guide leave and noticed just her car and the guests' car in the parking lot. At the conclusion of the tour, she bid farewell to the guests, stepped outside to wave them goodbye and watched them pull off down the drive. She had to finish closing up the doors so that the alarm would set properly.

As she was doing so, she suddenly heard voices from the old kitchen and into the adjoining modern kitchen, in the galley behind the locked door. She heard a male and a female discussing gardening from what she could tell and could hear the inflections and tones in their voices clearly, even though some of the words were mumbled and indiscernible. Immediately, Linda thought that for some reason the garden volunteers might have arrived. How they could get inside with no keys in a locked building and how they arrived without a car being seen in the lot was puzzling, but somehow, she thought, it must be them. But what if it was someone else? Linda knew that she had the option of encountering the people in the kitchen or calling the police, and she decided to approach them. If it were the gardeners, they would harmless. Their conversation wasn't frightening—just an everyday conversation. She wasn't walking into a hostile situation. She opened the doors with anticipation but saw no one standing in the galley. She looked around curiously, as the sounds of chatter had dissipated into the air around her. She was relieved that no one was there, and she vigilantly checked all doors once more and left wondering who she had just heard conversing in the homestead. Perhaps it was the friendly spirits of Nathan's brother and sister-in-law, John and Sarah, who called the place home for so many years.

The homestead is filled as well with haunting items, such as Nathan's silver shoe buckles, as bequeathed to Stephen Hempstead; his Yale roster, framed and hung inside an upstairs bedroom near his sister's room; his hunting musket; and his personal trunk, which once housed all its belongings. It is said that when the framed Yale roster was put inside the upstairs bedroom, it repeatedly fell off the wall for no reason, as if confused about its movement. After months, it ceased falling, but guests would stand in front of it, perhaps seeing the names Hale and Tallmadge or perhaps feeling its deep connection to Nathan, and would find themselves feeling faint just being near it.

To add to a haunting collection in the attic, there is a pair of unused coffins, as found by George Dudley Seymour just down the way from a chair that Seymour had built for President Taft on one of his visits to the property. He was just one of the famous visitors to the property—others included Eleanor Roosevelt and John Singer Sargent (who got stuck within a small hall between rooms due to his size and allegedly had to be buttered up and pushed out). Some insist that cameras start to malfunction around all the artifacts in the attic and do not allow proper photography to take place. It's a strange thing for the attic, but spirits are known to cause electronics to malfunction, so perhaps the energy is high up there.

As stated, the homestead is filled with stories. Investigators, mediums and all kinds of paranormal enthusiasts have signed up to spend hours in the homestead at night, following the creaks and moans, the apparitions, the shadows and the footsteps. Perhaps one of the most active rooms is the judgment room, home to the deacon's desk—a room where small court cases were heard and where Nathan's chair is placed. An authoritative figure, a person who is in charge of the homestead, has been felt by myself, sensitive and historian Jennifer Emerson and others. Indeed, Nathan's study Bible used to be housed in that very room as well.

Nathan Hale Schoolhouse in East Haddam, circa 2015.

The homestead is one of the most active Revolutionary haunts in the state, and the Hale legacy of ghostly phenomena has carried into the schoolhouses in both East Haddam and New London, which harbor their own accounts of paranormal activity.

Located right near a graveyard, it is hard to say which spirits may be haunting the small East Haddam schoolhouse, or perhaps Nathan finds himself visiting the location where he spent such brief time. With its beautiful views, it remains a spot where people come to learn about Nathan and his brief tenure there. An investigation within the East Haddam Schoolhouse was conducted alongside historian, sensitive and Seaside Shadows guide Robert Lecce; Sons of the American Revolution Connecticut Chapter property steward David Packard; myself; and my husband. The Revolutionary spirit was alive and well. Although it was at the end of the summer and otherwise warm, we immediately felt cool breezes passing through the small schoolhouse, and the candle flame flickered back and forth as if someone was moving past it. The candle sat on the long school table—did a student arrive? No, it felt like an adult. We saw shadowy movements and utilized our equipment to communicate: the SB7 Spirit Box, which utilizes radio waves to discern spirit voices, was turned on, as was an EVP recorder.

Robert and David spoke to the spirits of the local regiments and asked if any of them were part of a local regiment. The response was clear: "the Seventh." That was Nathan Hale's regiment. The male voice continued to speak, but clarity was hard to discern for a few segments of audio recording until Robert asked of the spirit if it knew who Benedict Arnold was. The response was clear and piercing: "Traitor." Suddenly, the spirit box indicated that there were more than a half a dozen members of the Seventh Regiment in the room, and they spoke of Hale with fondness. An electric feeling passed through all of us, as it was clear that we were speaking with those from the eighteenth century who knew we were also there to learn of them and their fellow colleague, Nathan Hale. At one point in the evening, the door burst open and winds picked up; an authoritarian presence entered. It was unclear who it might have been, but the presence commanded our attention and remains ingrained in each of our memories for its unique ability to absorb all the attention within the room.

In the fall months, our investigative group set forth to the New London Schoolhouse, to a city a bit more in Hale's favor, and this time we were accompanied by investigator Stacey Philips of DKS Paranormal and her son, Austin Mann, a spiritual intuitive. The schoolhouses had never been investigated, and as the evening began, all seemed quiet in New London. The schoolhouse is two floors high and not in its original location, having been moved like the one in East Haddam was. Once called the Union School, we hoped to make contact with any schoolmasters of years past.

On the first floor, we heard the trains roll by outside, the sounds of traffic horns and more, but no spirits. Robert, Austin, Stacey and I all felt that the spirits were upstairs, as we could hear their footsteps. We proceeded upstairs, where there were small electromagnetic fluctuations but still an eerie, deafening silence. David told us about a sketch rumored to be on the older walls, which had been burned—a student had drawn a ship with an eighteenth-century style. There was a small hole by the floor just big enough for an adult to fit through and crawl around to look for the drawing. Robert bravely embarked on this journey into the walls of the schoolhouse. Lo and behold, he found the ship. Of course, each one of us took a turn looking at the chalk-drawn ship on the wall, held there for hundreds of years and maybe drawn when Hale was the schoolmaster. The discovery of this etching livened the activity, and as we reconvened on the second floor of the schoolhouse, a shadowy apparition of an authoritative man once more

Nathan Hale Schoolhouse in New London on the evening of a paranormal investigation, circa 2015. *Photo by Martin J. Reardon Jr.*

made himself known. He was close to Austin and Robert, too, drawn more to the presence of men.

The shadow figure continued to follow the group around on the second floor. We moved again to the eerie silence of the first floor and then to the most active part of the schoolhouse as a whole: the basement, an archivist's treasure-trove of historical documents from the eighteenth and nineteenth centuries. There were portraits of Hale and pieces of wood from the original schoolhouse—some even burned from a fire that had one touched the schoolhouse—perhaps even some burned planks from the Burning of New London, during which the schoolhouse was spared almost in its entirety. Near this wood, Austin immediately saw the apparition of a man, also burned in his appearance, watchful, sad and attached to the stack of wood.

After we gawked and pored over the historical documents, it was time to speak with the spirits present. We shut off the lights and could barely see the outline of one another, lit only by the power lights of our equipment and the moonstone of my necklace. I walked around with the EMF and audio recorders in the dark near each investigator. We stood in a perfect circle around a small table, and as I walked around, I asked each investigator if he or she would like to ask a question. As I walked around, everyone participated except one, who was standing there quietly. "It's okay, it's late," I thought and carried on. We spent the rest of the night giving that investigator at the table space and walking around them. Apparition movements were seen around the room, and a trio of soldiers appeared behind Robert as if to walk him somewhere, yet that same investigator remained silent. Robert and the others witnessed as the trio gathered behind in a triangular manner. Unsure of their intent, we all began to feel uncomfortable. I turned on the lights. It was nearly one o'clock in the morning, and we all gasped as we looked to the end of the table where the silent group member had been. It was empty. No one stood there. We all saw the man and thought it was Marty, Austin, Robert or Dave's shadow; we all had walked around him.

We couldn't believe it. Someone was participating in the circle, but it was a spirit that had made himself known to each and every one of us. Robert did some research later and upon a visit to Shaw Mansion saw an old map of eighteenth-century New London. It showed the street where the schoolhouse now sits but hadn't then. That street had a row of buildings and was called "Jail Street," perhaps telling of prisoners? Whether it was a Patriot, someone injured in the Burning of New London or a prisoner is hard to tell, but men of distinct authority or immense personality were present in the schoolhouse that night. As a funny anecdote, we asked them about the Betsy Ross flag, and one of the few voice responses from the audio recorder we got that night told us that Betsy Ross was not the original American flag designer. Indeed, the spirit reminded us all that the American flag's first creator was Francis Hopkinson.

The homestead and two schoolhouses form the museums dedicated to Nathan Hale and his family's memory in the Constitution State. He was a man of honor. His is a legacy never to be forgotten. His is a spirit that continues to walk through his old stomping grounds alongside his friends and family in the colony of Connecticut that he so fondly called home.

FAIRFIELD

A PATRIOT HARBOR FOR FOUNDING FATHERS

BURR MANSION

Oftentimes, a town, much like a country or state, has founders. If residents of Fairfield were asked who their founding family was, the unequivocal answer given would be the Burrs. Thaddeus and Eunice Burr were often referred to as the "first family" of Fairfield during the late eighteenth century. They were looked up to by all the townspeople, had a great amount of wealth and also made a significant impact during the Revolution and beyond. Their efforts were clear and crucial to the development of the state of Connecticut as a colony and America as an independent and free nation.

The Burr Mansion was of immense importance during this time of revolution. Being a safe haven for rebel leaders, a wedding site for a Declaration signer, a resting place for the future first president and a political tool in a fiery raid, it seemed that there was no purpose the Burr Homestead didn't serve during the 1770s.

Thaddeus Burr was the grandson of Connecticut Colony's chief justice, Peter Burr, and son of Thaddeus Burr Sr., a deputy to the General Court in Hartford for Fairfield. Thaddeus Jr. was the lucky heir to high social ranking and Fairfield's most lucrative and expansive farming estate. He was educated at Yale, and while his trade was considered to be that of a farmer, it is widely acknowledged that he likely never worked or plowed his own fields but rather had staff and farmhands perform the entirety of the labor. He was a man of greatness and also a man of privilege. He married

Eunice Dennie, the then thirty-year-old daughter of the wealthy merchant Dennie family in town. The Burr family continued to move in the highest of social circles and networks throughout their lives. Thaddeus served in many distinguished roles during his time in Fairfield, including that of chief justice, sheriff, Council of Safety member, representative to the Connecticut General Assembly, first selectman and even a member of the Constitutional Convention. He was indeed one of Connecticut's presidential electors in 1789 who cast his vote for General George Washington to be president of the United States of America. Both Thaddeus and Eunice would go on to be key players in Revolutionary America just over a decade after their union.

Fairfield was considered to be a Patriot haven in a heavily Loyalist territory. Loyalists still inhabited parts of Fairfield right next to their rebel neighbors, but it was the safest place in the region that Patriots and their fellow supporters of the cause could inhabit. The Burrs were supporters and advocates of the Patriot cause, and Thaddeus was often away so that he could work on behalf of the fight for independence. A man of great means from his abundant crop export, his reach and influence were vast. He was also a man of diplomacy, and both he and his wife garnered a great deal of respect—at least for many years on both sides of the war. The Burrs greeted the likes of Benjamin Franklin, the Marquis de Lafayette, Governor Tryon and Dr. Timothy Dwight IV (eighth president of Yale), Samuel Adams, John Hancock and, last but not least, General George Washington. Washington frequently journeyed to and from Boston, and one of his favorite stops on the journey to rest his head and visit his friends was at the Burr Homestead in Fairfield.

Frank Samuel Child wrote in his account of the Burr Mansion in 1915 of the night that Sam Adams and John Hancock, along with their families, fled to the homestead of their good friend Thaddeus to seek refuge from the Loyalists in their pursuit: "It was about eight o'clock on the morning of April 22nd, 1775 that a messenger brought the news of Lexington [the Battles of Lexington and Concord] to Fairfield. The Honorably Thaddeus Burr, High Sheriff of the Country was standing on the porch of his mansion, discussing with Colonel Silliman and Mr. Jonathan Sturges the prospects of war."

The message was delivered to the trio by the horseman. The Burrs immediately made preparations, knowing that their Boston associates Hancock and Adams would soon be reaching out to them; they would be in need of safety.

In Boston, Paul Revere delivered the news of General Gage's march on Concord, and John Hancock and Samuel Adams were awakened suddenly

Burr Homestead in Fairfield, circa 1938. *Courtesy of the Library of Congress.*

and told that they needed to flee to escape the city if they wanted to survive. They had, after all, been masterminds of the cause and the war. The Loyalists would seek their capture first and foremost. Hancock's fiancée, Dorothy Quincy, was staying with his aunt Lydia and remained behind witnessing the chaos and the battle as it ensued on Lexington Green. The proverbial "shot heard 'round the world" had happened. Quincy's betrothed had to make his escape at night if he was to survive. They hid near a neighboring town, and the next day, Hancock's fiancée and aunt met up with them. Lydia Hancock, Dorothy Quincy, John Hancock and Samuel Adams all proceeded to Fairfield, Connecticut, and arrived at the home of the expectant Thaddeus and Eunice Burr, who welcomed them with open arms. The gentlemen's stay was brief. They knew that if they remained anywhere too long they would be found out and their plans foiled. They took off quickly to Philadelphia after a brief stay with the Burrs. The ladies stayed behind, safe at the hospitable homestead of the Burrs in Fairfield. Their stay was of some duration.

On June 28, 1775, General Washington came through Fairfield on his way toward Boston to take command of the Continental army. On his way, he stopped at none other than Burr Mansion to pay due respect to Thaddeus

Portrait of Samuel Adams as painted by John Singleton Copley, circa 1772. *Courtesy of Wikipedia.*

and Eunice. He had learned of their enormous efforts and of harboring of Ms. Hancock and Ms. Quincy—a noble and risky endeavor indeed. General Washington would be back the following year in April 1776, and so began his relationship with the Burr family.

By the summer following the Battles of Lexington and Concord, Hancock was becoming anxious to marry Ms. Quincy. His aunt seemed equally motivated to see the nuptials take place. After all, the esteemed and wealthy Hancock was marrying into another esteemed and wealthy family, the Quincys. Together they would be quite the powerful couple. On August 23, 1775, John Hancock and Dorothy Quincy wed at the Burr Homestead. As Hancock's carriage made its way through New York to the city of Fairfield on that humid, summer day, thousands of spectators lined the streets. He was one of the most honorable men in whose presence they would find themselves. Hancock was never a fan of such gestures but took his ride to Fairfield that day with the pride of knowing what a beautiful and outstanding woman he was about to wed. By his arrival in Fairfield, he was surrounded by his esteemed colleagues and welcomed into the Burr Mansion. Statesmen came across New England to witness the historic wedding day. The Burrs were ever the hospitable couple, always used to hosting the most exquisite and talked-about gatherings, parties and events. They made sure that the Hancocks wanted for nothing that day. The service was relatively brief, and the reception afterward was exciting. Residents of Fairfield surrounded the mansion and the yard around it just to get a glimpse of true elegance. Child wrote of the sights that the spectators beheld: "Silver buckles, white silk stockings, knee breeches of varied hues, scarlet vests and velvet coats with ruffled shirts and broad fine neckwear adorned the masculine fraternity while the ladies were radiant in silks and laces, lofty head-dress, resplendent jewelry and the precious heirlooms of old families."

Danger still lurked that day, as Hancock, then the second president of the Continental Congress, was still a wanted man. Local legend states that after the guests were provided their meals and refreshments, an alarm was sounded, and the entire Hancock family and bridal party left immediately.

Sadly, in April 1776, John Hancock's aunt passed away inside the Burr Mansion, having suffered from apoplexy (now often referred to as a stroke). The Burrs had a stone erected in her memory and marked her final resting place.

For months and years after the wedding, the Burrs continued to play host and entertainers to all number of guests from both sides of the war (mostly Patriots). Be it Governor Trumbull, General Washington, John Adams,

Portrait of John Hancock as painted by John Singleton Copley, circa 1765. *Courtesy of Wikipedia.*

Samuel Adams, Benjamin Franklin, Benjamin Tallmadge (Washington's right-hand man) or Thaddeus Burr's brother-in-law and Declaration signer Lyman Hall, they were the go-to homestead in all of Fairfield for the independence cause. They also had an air of professionalism to them and maintained respect from all sides throughout the war. Most notably, they often hosted the strong Loyalist governor of North Carolina, William Tryon. They hosted gatherings where all would dance and eat or drink together in peaceful manners, just as they would host private gatherings with their allies.

Happy history left the Burr Mansion in 1779. Thaddeus Burr was away on business, as he so often had to be for much of the war, leaving Eunice alone, when the Burning of Fairfield at the hands of British troops destroyed hundreds of the structures in the town of Fairfield, including ninety-seven homes, sixty-seven barns, forty-eight stores, two schools, a county jail, two meetinghouses and a courthouse. The day was July 7. A warning was sent from the nearby fort at Black Rock that the British had been spotted dropping anchor by the Fairfield coast. Hastily, although this came without anticipation, the Fairfield residents began to prepare their defenses and hide all personal belongings of any importance or worth, including livestock, silver and household goods. Some took the job of protecting assets, while others took the duty of defending their homes.

The raid did not come until later in the afternoon. The British disembarked from their vessels at McKenzie's Point and marched down the beach there. They were under the command of General George Garth and also General Tyron, the very governor whom the Burrs had hosted generously on more than one occasion. The British set up headquarters while the locals set up their defense at Round Hill. Some Fairfield residents thought that their safety and the safety of their buildings would be ensured due to their amicable relationship with Tryon. He had, in fact, given certain buildings—such as churches, ministry housing and the Burr Homestead—protection. This protection seemed to be meaningless, as the British burned down virtually every building, "protected" or not, and brutally killed local residents who resisted. Tryon had even met with Mrs. Burr to discuss her protection earlier in the day. She watched helplessly as she heard the gunshots and watched the flames roar in destruction of her town. It wasn't until late that evening that she was shocked to have the British on her doorstep.

When the dozen or so British men arrived at the Burr Homestead, Mrs. Eunice Burr explained the protective order that she had received from General Tryon. According to Mrs. Burr, the men retorted in shouts and exclaimed, "Tryon be damned!"

They violently tore her protective order from her hands and shredded it to pieces in front of her. They then demanded information about her husband. They wanted to know where he was and desired any papers he might have in the house. She refused to give them any information, no matter how they would choose to torture her. She continued to act in dignity and explained herself and the homestead's unique position in the town accurately and efficiently. She made a compelling plea for the safety of the mansion. The British were not interested in hearing it and continued in their unwarranted act of violence toward Mrs. Burr. General Tryon was nowhere to be found, and these men knew that and did not follow whatever code of ethics he may or may not have told them applied. They physically assaulted Mrs. Burr, grabbing her and stripping the buttons off her dress, exposing her in her undergarments. They stole the silver buckles from her shoes, as well as items they found of value in her home, and destroyed all her belongings, such as mirrors, furniture and more, right in front of her.

The brave Mrs. Burr watched in horror as they destroyed everything she and her husband had created. While some men looted her home, others tried haphazardly to rip the remainder of her clothes off her body, stripping her naked and trying to rob her of her dignity. In this they failed. They threw her on the ground to more easily find any items of worth on her person. They took her watch, a precious family heirloom, and gold buttons on the sleeves of her dress by her wrists and sent her fleeing into the meadow and woods near the property, fearing for her life. Their pursuit of her was brief, as they returned to set fire to the homestead, burning it and all that was left within to the ground. She hid in the thickets until the soldiers were out of sight. When she emerged from the brush, she went to the aid of the injured, the devastated and the helpless to do what she could. Eunice was able to explain every event of that day in detail during her testimony in a postwar deposition. She remained a woman of complete honor in the face of those Loyalists' every effort to take that away from her. Eunice Dennie Burr had remained dedicated and steadfast to both her husband and the cause in the face of unspeakable horror.

This was not the end of the Burrs' legacy by any means. As you can see, there is a Burr Mansion that remains in the center of Fairfield today. That Burr Mansion is in the very same spot as the one that suffered in the destruction that day. The foundation and basement are from the original mansion that stood on that site. The one that stands now was also built by Thaddeus and Eunice Burr. For years after the Burning of Fairfield, the Burrs had made their home elsewhere in Fairfield and continued to host the likes of Hancock and other Revolutionary icons. On one of Hancock's visits, he chatted with the couple and explained his idea that they rebuild their home. He even offered to assist in the financing and the design of the structure so that it would resemble his own house and mansion in Boston. Thaddeus took to this idea enthusiastically. The new Greek Revival–style mansion was completed in 1791 by architect and carpenter Daniel Dimon and his team of men. The property had still remained in the Burr family since the mid-1600s. The new mansion was built to have a high gambrel roof and dormer windows, large rooms with high joints, a great hall and generous glass in the door to let in even more light on the glorious interior. Much of the inside is of Italianate and classical design.

Both Thaddeus and Eunice carried out the remainder of their lives in the mansion, filling it with as many new items to match the times and the family as they could. In some ways, their home's legacy began anew in 1791. Thaddeus went on to assume his role as town representative after the burning, and that was when he subsequently became part of the state convention to ratify the U.S. Constitution. Eunice dedicated much of her later years to the importance of educating young women alongside young men and established the private school Fairfield Academy. It became a premier coeducational institution of influence throughout the region.

Theirs is a colorful history, full of beautiful weddings and violent acts. The Burr property has seen much, and what a guest list the home has played host to as well. The Burr Mansion, which is now operated by the Fairfield Museum and History Center, is a breathtaking sight to behold. It still serves as a favorite wedding spot in western Connecticut. You can get married in the same place as John Hancock and Dorothy Quincy. It's safe to say, however, that there would be guests of the spiritual kind at your wedding as well. True, it may seem that the homestead is rather quiet these days, remaining usually vacant except for special events. However, the Burrs are still calling their iconic mansion home.

Paranormal investigation took place for the first time in Burr Homestead history in the spring of 2015. Central Connecticut State University's Society of Paranormal Research, the New England Spiritual Team Inc. and Elisabeth Angel Pfeifer, spirit photographer/physical empath, accompanied me and my husband to see what spiritual interactions we might encounter at the historic haunt. Armed with a plethora of equipment, the New England Spiritual Team Inc. had everything from audio recorders to a variety of electromagnetic field detectors, namely something referred to as a REM pod. The evening's journey brought most of the assembled down to the basement, within the very foundation that stood prior to the home's rebuilding in 1791 and was there for the Burning of Fairfield. As we entered into the rear of the expansive basement and went near a doorway (assumed to go to the outside but found out later to be built around), the smell of smoke seemed to fill the air. We weren't expecting to have that sensation creep up so quickly, but it

Burr Homestead (aka Burr Mansion) in Fairfield, circa 2015. *Photo by Martin J. Reardon Jr.*

did. From there on out, the evening was nothing short of eventful. A female presence was detected by the basement fireplace, also thought to be original to the homestead, and was heard by the sensitives present to be saying, "I told him not to go. I told him it wouldn't be safe."

It's hard to say who this may have been, but could it have been Eunice speaking of Thaddeus prior to the Burning of Fairfield in 1779? It stands to reason that it just might be. The group of investigators took the opportunity to split up throughout the large mansion to make sure that all areas were investigated thoroughly. I remained in the basement for a time alongside Elisabeth and my husband, Marty. We were equipped with the audio recorders, the REM pod and cameras. Elisabeth, a seasoned investigator with the gift of spirit photography, began to take photos rapidly around the room. As a spirit medium, I told her that I sensed a gentleman figure present, as if he was invited to some kind of event and was extending his hand out graciously to me as if we were just meeting. Immediately, Elisabeth snapped a photo of me. Sure enough, in the image a shadow is cast on the wall behind me, but it is not mine, as the dark basement let no light in. It is that of a man with his hair tied back by a ribbon, broad shouldered in apparent uniform, extending his hand out as expected. Just the next week, Elisabeth and I went to retrieve this miraculous photo, which everyone in the group had seen, but it had vanished. In fact, many photos from Elisabeth's high-tech camera would go on to vanish mysteriously after that night.

Moving into another area of the basement, seemingly led by the gracious gentleman, we arrived at a storage area. It is unclear what it would have been in the 1700s, but there were multiple doorways leading into it. As we stood there asking the apparent spirit questions, a loud *bang* was heard on the opposite side of the basement. Marty left the back room to ascertain what the noise was and determine if was another investigator. He found out later that it was not—no one was even remotely close the vicinity from which the noise had come. It seemed a decoy—a way to get Marty out of the room. Less than a minute after his departure, the stationary REM pod—which had not illuminated or made a sound that indicated any fluctuation in electromagnetic fields or manipulation by a spirit responding to us since our arrival—suddenly lit up nearly all four colors (red, blue, yellow and green) all at once. Sound effects indicating that it was being touched by a hand emanated in the night air and echoed throughout the basement.

We watched in awe as it responded to our questions. Then suddenly, I heard Elisabeth shriek in horror and in pain. "Get out of my head," she exclaimed. She felt immense pain rushing through her and stated that the spirit might have had some kind of head injury in his life that she was sensing. The pain was excruciating and too much for her to take. She left the room, and I stayed with the gentleman spirit. The EMF fluctuations and responses continued for a time, but it was soon time to reconvene to other parts of the house. Just before we departed the basement, the audio recorders indicated something strange. The sounds of a piano were playing in the background of our discussion trying to ascertain the sounds the REM pod was making. We proceeded throughout the three remaining floors of the house, and everyone experienced different sensations. Some saw shadows or apparitions, and others felt physically all too close to the spirits and had to sit down for a break. The REM pod went off just once more on the first floor in one of the likely parlor rooms near the front entrance. Phantom sounds echoed, the walls knocked and verbal cues were given that the Burr Mansion was unquestionably alive with spirit activity.

If you are ever so lucky to visit the Burr Mansion, allow the eminence to surround you. Try to breathe in the history of all those who walked the very grounds and halls before you—those who forged a nation centuries ago. Spirits of historic figures long since passed still seem to view the Burr Homestead as a welcome refuge and a home for their rebel ideas, important discussion and unforgettable social gatherings.

SUN TAVERN

Less than half a mile down Old Post Road in Fairfield, look at the breathtaking historical array of structures on the old Fairfield Town Green. Another stunning Colonial, eighteenth-century gambrel-roofed structure may capture your eye. Restored in the 1970s by the indomitable and masterful William Lee and his wife, the once grand but somehow fallen structure was brought back to life. William and Anne Lee would go on to call this building home for a number of years during the restoration as William, the town historian of Fairfield, brought to light the true story of what had once stood within the walls of this colonial structure. This building is today affectionately referred to as the Sun Tavern, but upon reconstruction shortly after the Burning of Fairfield in 1779, the tavern maintained its name, after creator Samuel Penfield, and was called Penfield's Rising Sun Tavern. Mr. Lee would go on to chronicle the entire history and restoration in his book *The Sun Tavern and the Red Admiral.*

Samuel Penfield was another man of means and wealth in Fairfield; however, he also lost both his home and business at the hands of Tryon's Loyalists in 1779. His tavern stood as it does today, not far from Burr Mansion during the Revolution, as a Patriot meeting place and thus a target. George Washington's Papers, as archived by the Library of Congress, indicate a receipt that he stayed at Penfield's in Fairfield from April 11 to April 12, 1776. The building would later perish in the Burning of Fairfield, becoming yet another icon that would eventually make its way back to the Fairfield Town Green.

After the devastation of that summer day in 1779, Penfield was ready to rebuild. Armed with ambition, funds and the assistance of his good friend Thaddeus Burr, Penfield would bring immense contributions to the restoration of his proud and beautiful town. Before the Burning of Fairfield, Penfield had been living in the former homestead of the pastor Reverend John Jones of the First Congregational Church, right on the border of the town green. This very plot would become the perfect site for a tavern. In fact, a tavern had been on the list of priorities given by the town of Fairfield as to buildings that needed to be reconstructed as soon as possible. Penfield and his associates quickly got his affairs in order and legalities ensured, and construction of the Sun Tavern was soon underway.

There had previously been a tavern on the town green that catered more to the Loyalist population, but Penfield's would be different. His would serve the Patriots, the independent and free American people. The architecture was basic, and the tavern was built with five large rooms, all equipped with high ceilings, giving it a much grander feel. There was a hallway of great width and a staircase to a third-floor lounge-type facility, perfect for any kind of social gathering. In addition, there was a cellar for wine and a bar so that spirits of the non-supernatural kind could flow freely for all who paid the tavern a visit. The property was more extensive than the current landscape may show today. In the late eighteenth and early nineteenth centuries, the tavern would have been accompanied by numerous barns and outbuildings and/or sheds. A tavern of the day was not just for drinking after all—it was a place for planning and meeting, a place where travelers from all walks of life might lay their heads to spend the night and a place of boarding. Penfield's tavern became such a bustling hot spot that he was rarely home with his wife and children in the home they had rebuilt. Instead, he was pivotal to the Patriot reconstruction of a nation via this tavern.

Just months after General George Washington was inaugurated as the first official United States president, he made a trip to Fairfield to see how his friends were faring, how the city he had grown to know so well the decade prior was recovering and rebuilding and to have a nice and hearty rest in one of the early New England towns of which he had grown so fond. The Burr Mansion had not yet been rebuilt for his 1789 visit, and that was where he had always stayed in the past. It stands to reason that there was only one place in town where he could stay the night: Penfield's Rising Sun Tavern.

There are a few skeptics who question if Washington may have spent the night here; however, historian Bill Lee and the residents of Fairfield know that in the town of 1789, it was quite literally the only place that the president could have spent the night, and his documentation of his stay leads many to infer references to the Sun Tavern. It was October 1789 when President George Washington and his entourage, consisting of two aides and six servants, arrived in Fairfield. Washington described the purpose of his visit to one of his favorite Connecticut stomping grounds in a letter to his sister, in which he wrote that his journey was "by way of relaxation from business and re-establishing my health."

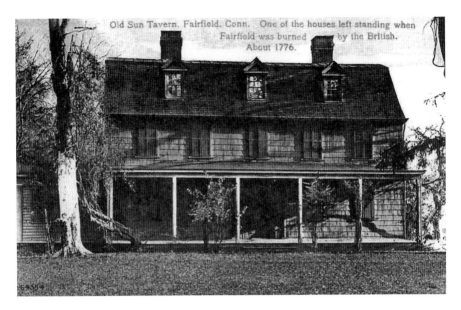

Old Sun Tavern in Fairfield as depicted in an early twentieth-century postcard, circa 1910. *Courtesy of Wikipedia.*

Washington did journal throughout his stay about the abundance of the farmland in Fairfield and how impressed he was with their decade-long recovery: "From hence to Fairfield where we dined and lodged is 12 miles [from Norwalk area]; and part of it is very rough road, but not equal to that thro' Horse Neck. The superb Landscape, however, which is to be seen from the meeting house of the latter is a rich regalia. We found all the farmers busily employed gathering, grinding, and expressing the Juice of their apples; the crop of which they say is rather above mediocrity."

Fairfield, it seemed, was thriving and proved a welcome rest for President Washington. The president ultimately departed in the morning at "sunrise" on the main highway, which is exactly where the tavern was located. Washington had also noted that he had become acquaintances with Mr. Penfield over a decade earlier, nearer the beginning of the American Revolution, in 1776. It seems that President Washington would have stayed with his old friend and fellow Patriot Samuel.

The Fairfield Museum and History Center's archives indeed include documentation from at least one resident at the time of Washington's visit who remembered seeing him arrive via coach with all his men and all the residents gathering in the street. The story was retold annually by the townsfolk in great celebration of this triumphant visit.

A few decades after the president's visit to dear Fairfield, Mr. Penfield passed away. Afterward, the tavern just did not have the same air and ambience to it and ultimately closed its doors as a place of boisterous events, important guests and sociable outings. The tavern was converted into a single-family home, which it remained for more than one hundred years before the property fell into disrepair and was saved by town historian and architect William Lee, who had established Lee Associates Art for Architecture in 1954, touched many historic homes throughout his career and fought triumphantly for the salvage of the Rising Sun Tavern. History like that can certainly never be replaced, and that was evident to Mr. Lee immediately upon his viewing of the property.

Bill Lee's relationship with the Fairfield Sun Tavern would seem to be fated from the moment he set eyes on it. Even numerous other people quite knowledgeable of the people of Fairfield's past told Mr. Lee over the years that he closely resembled Samuel Penfield—an uncanny likeness, as if Penfield himself in some way came back to resurrect the tavern. But Bill Lee's passions and talents were also all his own, and as he so humbly states, he could not have accomplished it without the support of his beautiful and fabulous wife, Anne. In 1953, years before Bill Lee would take his architectural prowess to the tavern, it was suggested to him by friends that he take a look at the poor condition of the Sun Tavern. This was shortly after he had drawn a detailed map of colonial Fairfield.

Bill went to the old tavern the day after his friends' request, saw its disrepair and wished to be able to fix it right then and there. The tavern's needs never left his head from that day forward. Bill also wrote that it seemed as though the tavern was waiting for him: "I stopped for a moment looking at this abandoned, once-famous Tavern that seemed to scream out its past history to me. With its questionable future and impressive image, I took a few photographs of it. As I was walking away I had a strange feeling someone was up in those windows watching me as I left."

Perhaps it was Penfield looking down at his successor, a man with incomparable talent. Bill Lee went on to work in varying capacities for the Town of Fairfield, assisting in planning the bicentennial, historical research and a variety of important duties. When discussing the Sun Tavern in the 1970s with First Selectman John Sullivan, it was decided that budgetary allotments would be made for the historic property's renovations and that Mr. Lee and his wife would subsequently rent it out and care for the property. This is exactly what they did. Lee assisted in the rehabilitation of the place, and by October 1979, he and Anne had moved in together. Their children were grown, and this was a unique chapter in their marriage and journey with each other.

Bill wrote, "Unpredictable circumstances and destiny somehow brought us there. Our sudden and seemingly easy occupancy was a pleasurable experience. With our family, friends and neighbors, we immediately felt comfortably at home. After two centuries of wear and abuse, the Sun Tavern was saved." Little did Bill know that his spiritual and sometimes supernatural journey with Sun Tavern had only just begun.

It was shortly after his and Anne's arrival to the home on a sunny afternoon that Bill decided to take a drive to Independence Hall to retrieve his mail. Upon Bill's arrival, the parking lot at the town hall was full. The location of the closest road was near where the Fairfield Museum is now, but at that time, the spot was vacant. Bill had to go elsewhere to find a parking spot that late afternoon. This had never happened to him before. He carried on down the little road where the museum would come to be and back up to Beach Road but, alas, still no parking spaces. What an odd day. Bill continued to drive, letting fate take the wheel as he muttered, "Jeez, I can't believe there's

Penfield's Rising Sun Tavern as restored on the town green in Fairfield, photograph circa 2015. *Photo by Martin J. Reardon Jr.*

no place to park." Just down the road, he arrived at a grassy spot where he could pull up and park.

As he pulled to the grassy area on the street, he noticed that it was the Old Burying Ground, a popular burial site in eighteenth century and the cemetery where he knew Samuel Penfield was buried. He parked at the farthest side of the grass, preparing to indulge himself in a little stroll through the cemetery. He knew from charts that Sam Penfield's stone was approximately near the northern side of the burial ground. He climbed over the stone wall and began his quest to find Penfield's resting place. The grass was tall, forcing him to sometimes look a little harder to uncover the names, and some stones were broken, fallen or decayed from age. He figured out where he should be going and arrived about halfway through the cemetery but did not find Penfield. The day just kept getting stranger, it seemed, but he continued to walk around. After a long time had passed and the sun was beginning to go down, Bill decided that it was time to go. He would find Penfield another day. He turned around once more for one final glance, and his eyes were immediately drawn to his shadow on the ground in front of him—so tall and outstretched under the setting sun casting shadows throughout the burying ground. And where did his shadow lead? To none other than Samuel Penfield's stone. His shadow went right up the entirety of Penfield's stone, selecting that stone alone. "Boom, right there when I was ready to leave, there was my shadow on Penfield's stone," Lee recollected. "And that's the truth, and I do believe there's something to that."

Penfield made his watchful presence increasingly known from that point forward. The "Red Admiral" in Lee's book title refers to the famous butterfly by that name and also to the most haunting yet comforting spiritual experience he and his wife, Anne, had during their stay at Sun Tavern. During renovations, Bill created a small bluestone patio area, utilizing all stones found on the Sun Tavern's property. The patio was furnished, and floral arrangements were aptly placed outside. It was the perfect place for Bill and Anne to relax—he noted that Anne always had a book in hand as an avid and enthusiastic reader. What better place to put up your feet with a good book than on this picturesque patio? It seemed that every time they chose to sit on the patio, a single butterfly would appear, completely untraditional in its appearance. Bill wrote, "It had a rapid flight pattern, flying extremely fast, making a very noticeable fluttering sound. It would suddenly land on the nearby table or chairs and occasionally land on Anne or myself."

One afternoon, as the butterfly fluttered about in its usual manner, it landed delicately on the pages of Anne's book, seemingly a member of the group. "Bill, look at our friend the butterfly," Anne remarked. Penfield was always picking interesting ways to communicate with them and let them know that he was there in an approving and friendly matter, and this time was no different. Anne continued, "Look at what the book says below him." Cautiously and quietly, Bill approached the book and read the words: "Sam has planned to return." From then on, they named the butterfly, whose species is known as the Red Admiral, Samuel Penfield and considered the butterfly's visits to be the visits of the Sun Tavern's founder, Patriot Samuel Penfield. Indeed, they might be right, as butterflies are often considered a sign from the heavens that a spirit is nearby, watching over and giving a pleasant nod of approval. Penfield's spirit was always around and always had good intent.

Certainly there are other times when a spirit's presence may be a bit unsettling, and in an old house full of creaks and moans, there are moments when it's hard to discern whether it's a natural sound or a spirit making itself known. One evening, in the L-shaped room close to the front door, which still had the original doors when the Lees called it home, there was an odd occurrence. The ell was where food was prepared back in the day, and that evening, as they sat down to relax after dinner for some reading, they listened to the wind blowing and howling outside. They were safe inside the warm walls of the old tavern turned homestead. The original door still had old latches and a strap hinge. Suddenly, there was the sound of the latch tapping back and forth, and it didn't sound like the wind anymore. It sounded like someone was outside in the wicked wind trying to get inside for cover. They watched as the latch moved and tapped, rapping back and forth for a few moments before it silenced. Peering out the window, they discovered that no one was outside. Maybe it was the wind after all, or maybe it was an old visitor from centuries ago arriving at the tavern for lodging and a drink.

Similarly, on another occasion, Bill and Anne witnessed a door off the pantry in the bathroom area slowly creak open all on its own at about ten o'clock at night. As the door opened, Bill and Anne watched with anticipation to see what or who might enter. There was silence, no more sounds. Bill, being an architect, said, "Maybe it was a heat change, a draft, the weight of the door—it's an old house! But you never know." It was one of those not-so-rare occurrences that folks in old New England homes throughout Connecticut experience—always unsure if it is the bones of the house or if it's a previous resident or visitor still walking the halls; perhaps the paths of the living and the dead crossed, if even for only a moment. The Lees left the Sun Tavern after fifteen years of calling their reconstructed bit of history home. It was time to move on, and sadly, Anne has since passed. Bill remains town historian emeritus of Fairfield at the time of this publication and continues to produce beautiful paintings, works of art depicting western Connecticut in era of times past and the spectacular landscapes that surround it today.

Fairfield was a Patriot stronghold in Loyalist terrain and host to the most notable heroes of the Revolutionary War. From Thaddeus and Eunice Burr to Samuel Penfield, they provided safety, refuge and hospitality to the likes of John Hancock, Samuel Adams, George Washington and many more. The Burrs were trusted in the wedding of a Declaration signer and the hosting of his loved ones, given refuge after the Battles of Lexington and Concord. Eunice proved to be one of the strongest women Revolutionary Connecticut would come to see. Samuel Penfield contributed to the revival of Fairfield, making the statement that the British burning in 1779 would be far from the end of Fairfield. If any city in Connecticut could house the spirits of such Revolutionary notables, Fairfield may indeed be it. Maybe if you walk the halls of Burr Mansion, you'll hear Mr. or Mrs. Hancock chatting with Thaddeus and Eunice. Or, if you step foot inside the old Sun Tavern, you'll see the Red Admiral and know that Penfield is smiling down upon you.

LEBANON

THE CONTINENTAL ARMY'S CONNECTICUT BASE

LEBANON WAR OFFICE

In rural eastern Connecticut lies a small, red Colonial structure, two stories high and overlooking the Lebanon Green. A historic New England building on a sleepy street, it may capture your eye for its eighteenth-century architecture but otherwise holds the appearance of an antique, red clapboard building of modest size. A small sign hangs outside, the only indication that there may be something more to this well-kept and interesting building. That sign reads, "Lebanon War Office." The Lebanon War Office, just up the road from the Governor Trumbull House and museum, was unequivocally one of the most pivotal places, meetinghouses and storage facilities in the entire Revolutionary War. The Lebanon War Office construction date is not known with exact certainty, mostly because the purpose for which it was built was not officially to be a war office, meeting room or even a homestead but rather a storage facility for the merchant Trumbull family, based in Lebanon.

Some believe that it was the first Governor Trumbull's father who had the building constructed; however, the style of the building is more suited to the 1760s, which lends itself to being constructed by Governor Trumbull Sr. rather than his father. Both the governor-to-be and his father were merchants and wholesalers and lived in Lebanon, Connecticut, not far from where the Lebanon War Office is located by the green today. However, both the Governor Trumbull House and War Office have been moved small distances to the area of West Town Street, where they are located today. Being in the merchant and wholesale business and on the direct trade path between the port of Norwich and Hartford, the Trumbulls required a storage facility, and that is what the War Office was built to be: a warehouse facility with a small office for Governor Trumbull and his family to conduct business.

When the American Revolution began in 1775 and shots were fired at Bunker Hill, Lebanon's involvement was immediately clear. The Lebanon militiamen, who became quite renowned in the Continental army, were among the first out-of-state troops to arrive to help Massachusetts colony. It was then that Governor Trumbull volunteered the use of his storehouse as a meeting place. The first Continental Congress sent a request that a Council of Safety be set up in each colony, and Trumbull's storage facility in Lebanon would become the official meeting place of this ordained Council of Safety in Connecticut. The Council of Safety would convene to address day-to-day operations of the state, including emergencies. Committees of Safety worked alongside Councils of Safety at this juncture to take care of similar measures at a town, rather than state, level. It was in 1775 when a mere warehouse would be turned into an official war office that would see one of the largest collections of founding fathers and notable Revolutionary military figures.

Whenever legislature wasn't in session, the Council of Safety ran the show. As the official representation of each colony, they assumed the colony's responsibilities, including recruiting troops, supplying troops, clothing troops, determining where forts and ships would be built, finding sites in which to gather supplies and more. The past president of the Connecticut Sons of the American Revolution explained the importance of the Lebanon War Office during the forging of a nation, saying, "The Lebanon War Office was the Pentagon of Connecticut during the American Revolution."

Lebanon took the lead in meeting places of a fledgling nation. Lebanon residents were, for the most part, ardent supporters of the colonists, the Sons of Liberty and the forming of the Continental army—much more than other towns. This political support from locals made the Lebanon War Office an incredibly safe place to hold meetings of such pertinence. Shaw noted as well that of the more than 1,100 council meetings during the entire war, more than half were within the very walls of the Lebanon War Office.

There was no time to waste. As soon as the Lebanon War Office became a meeting place for the Council of Safety and for war planning, a request came from Boston. The Siege in Boston was taking place in the beginning of the war, and the Lexington alarm had been sounded. Washington sent a request to Lebanon for two tons of gunpowder. Two tons is now and was

Lebanon War Office, circa 1938. *Courtesy of the Library of Congress.*

then a tall order that a war office in rural Connecticut wasn't sure it could fulfill. The colonial fighters needed this for muskets and cannons, as the British had surrounded all areas of Dorchester Heights. There was a real shortage of gunpowder, and in Lebanon, the governor and Council of Safety members were afraid that they couldn't deliver. They also had concerns as to repercussions, as the war was just beginning. As Sons of American Revolution member and historic house expert Stephen Marshall noted, "They were going up against the largest dynasty in the world [England] with colonies all over the world. America was the largest colonized country."

Whether the war was won or lost by the Patriots or the Tories, the effects would be vast, and the early American country they had once known would be permanently changed. Each state had to support its own and Connecticut already required weaponry, but this was one of the first of its kind: a federal order.

The council convened to determine what the colony of Connecticut needed and what the colonial soldiers needed, as well as how they could serve both. That ultimately would be the largest duty the council would serve throughout the duration of the war. The council did the best it could to comply with Washington's request and order and was ultimately able to acquire one ton of gunpowder and send it up to Boston to assist its comrades in combatting British seizure. How did rural Connecticut come up with so much gunpowder? Simple, really: Governor Trumbull and the Trumbull family had spent a lifetime building relationships with merchants all over the colonies, gaining respect and influence. This merchant network would be the lifeline of the war office and for the Continental army as a whole.

As the Sons of the American Revolution Connecticut noted, they were able to supply provisions beyond compare, including tents, utensils, iron pots, wooden bowls, canteens, clothing, blankets, flints, ammunition, powder, beef, pork and more to state militia units and naval ships. Connecticut was coined officially as the "Provision State" during the centennial in 1876, an acknowledgement of its large contribution to the American Revolution via its ability to supply the troops. Provisions were a major, if not the most important, purpose of war office coordination; however, it was far from being the only purpose for which the office was accountable. *Hartford Courant* journalist Dave Altimari wrote, "The council's duties were mostly to insure that supplies were getting to both Connecticut and other colonial troops. It was also responsible for housing any captured prisoners, dealing with economic issues and overseeing the state's fledgling Navy, which consisted of 13 commissioned ships that protected the state's coastline."

Where exactly did these ships come from? They were commissioned by the council after a decision was made and came from all over the state— notably in the region, ships came from Essex, Old Saybrook, East Hampton, East Haddam, Norwich, New London and Groton. Forts were also forged on council orders and named in council meetings, such as the aforementioned Fort Griswold and Fort Trumbull. Fort Trumbull was, of course, named after Governor Jonathan Trumbull Sr. and Fort Griswold after the deputy governor of the administration, Matthew Griswold.

Eastern Connecticut was a stronghold for colonial belief, and some of the pre-Revolutionary era may have even considered it a geographical strong hold for radical belief. However, it was this very attitude that made the area around Lebanon War Office crucial to the success of the nation as whole. So, who exactly attended these meetings with the governor and his council over the years? Attendants included the likes of William Williams, Declaration signer who lived across the street; Samuel Huntington, Continental Congress president from 1789 to 1781 and Declaration signer, who served as a scribe and secretary of the council; the Marquis de Lafayette, the French officer who fought with and led the Continental army during the American Revolution; Henry Knox, soldier and the first United States secretary of war; and even General George Washington, the future first president of the United States of America. Other distinguished military officers included Israel Putnam, Samuel Holden Parsons, Jedediah Huntington, Major General Joseph Spencer, Francois Jean de Beauvoir (Marquis de Chastellux), Armand Louis de Gontaut, Duc de Lauzun and Jean-Baptiste Donatien de Vimeur de Rochambeau, commander in chief of the French Expeditionary Force sent to assist in the Revolution. What a guest log indeed for the powerful Lebanon War Office.

As far as notable meetings, there were too many to narrow down. The request for gunpowder during the Siege of Boston was one of the most notable inaugural meetings of the house. Perhaps, though, one of the most memorable experiences for the gentlemen who met at the Lebanon War Office occurred when a draft of the Declaration of Independence arrived before it was even signed by all parties. The copy arrived at the war office only four or five days after it was approved. The Council of Safety members decided that the matter was too important at that time to decide on and tabled the Declaration for the entire summer, until the legislature was back in session in October. Then the matter of the Declaration became the first order of business. It was the council's duty to review the Declaration and inform the town and the general public of the surrounding area of its contents.

The most talked-about meeting attendee would be General Washington, who usually found himself in areas such as Hartford or New Haven for meetings and not usually in the route of Lebanon. However, in the spring of 1781, on his way to Newport to review the French troops preceding their long march to Yorktown, the Virginia general found himself planning the large culminating trip and subsequent battle with the governor and Council of Safety of Connecticut. They planned his trip and continued coordination of Lauzun's Legion, which consisted of French army and navy troops and volunteers who supported the American effort who were necessary assets and contributors to American success in the Battle at Yorktown.

Washington and others agreed that the cavalry was to spend the winter of 1780–81 at winter quarters in Lebanon. The troops stayed with their horses in barracks built on the Trumbull property. Other troops lived with their families in houses surrounding the Lebanon Town Green. With French troops in town and the height of the Revolution in progress, the population of Lebanon grew from 1,500 to nearly 4,000. After the Revolution, the population diminished back to its original size once more. More than 200 French troops had occupied the Lebanon Green; this would provide a distraction. When French troops traveled through Connecticut, they would go through Lebanon but eventually travel back through Middletown, down to New Haven and along the coastline. Meanwhile, the left flank formation was moved through the Hartford area. To have Lauzun's Legion in Lebanon would be a distraction in case the British decided to attack through Connecticut and thwart the main French troops located in areas such as Hartford. Their time in Lebanon was pivotal to serving this distraction.

Local legend asserts that there were a few Frenchmen executed and buried around the Lebanon Green—two for attempting desertion and one who became famous for his nontraditional death. Some believe that he stole a pig from the locals for sustenance, but others participating in town gossip insisted that the very same French soldier got in trouble for courting one of the local ladies he was not supposed to court, wooing her and perhaps having some kind of inappropriate relations with her. That very man, whose name was not documented, was said to have been executed for his crimes and is buried not far from the current site of the Lebanon War Office. Some believe that if anyone haunts the Lebanon green, it would be this French soldier, there to support the Continental army yet killed by its very supporters. Others believe the Lebanon Green to be filled with spirits—many of those the souls of the French in Lauzun's Legion who wintered there and passed away or, worse yet, were executed and whose bodies remain there to this day.

By the time Washington arrived in Lebanon the following spring, plans had been made regarding the town's assistance to accompany him under Rochambeau in Yorktown in the following months. The French from Newport and from parts of Connecticut traveled down to the Battle at Yorktown, where the French navy successful coordinated a blockade on the British in Virginia. The Continental army and French troops met decisive victory in Yorktown after much coordination, begun nearly a year earlier in Lebanon. For Washington's brief stay in Lebanon, he found accommodation at the home of future governor Jonathan Trumbull Jr. near the office.

Exactly where they met is clear, and much of the building was still often used for storage. Stephen Shaw, Stephen Marshall and historians noted that the fireplaces built into the structure faced toward one-third of the building, leaving the rest likely for cold storage; it is indeed that one-third that you can enter today to view the museum, as it is run by the Connecticut Sons of the American Revolution. It is believed that for this one-third of the building, the downstairs was used as the meeting room, and the room above it was used as a type of quarters where one could stay the night, be it a soldier or meeting attendee. Those would be the only two rooms that would be heated for such purposes.

The upstairs divide between sleeping quarters and storage room was clear, and you can still see the old chalk lettering above the upstairs doorway between the two rooms that says, "Door." There are other chalk drawings throughout the second-floor storage area indicating where certain goods would be kept and how they were counted. Why white chalk? That's what would show up when navigating by candlelight to make it clear where you were on a dark evening. There was a trick, however: the staircase that sits there today to provide easy access did not exist in the eighteenth century. The only way to get in was through a trapdoor, and that's where they hauled the goods upstairs for storage as well. They also hid something else underneath their stored goods: king's wood, floorboards wider than eighteen inches that would keep them hidden from the Patriot masterminds below. Pieces of king's wood, clay pipes and original eighteenth-century window sashes were all found during the 2015 renovation.

Utilizing old Roman numerals and scribes from millers, Marshall and the crew knew exactly how to place floor joists and followed the original alignment of the property as closely as possible. Marshall's renovations and restorations were completed in 2015 and included the original chimney and fireplace, as well as resurrecting the feel of the war office as it once stood. The office would go on to have many lives after this, becoming everything from a town library to a post office and a family homestead that saw the birth of a child within the home in the late nineteenth century. The property slowly fell into disrepair after Governor Trumbull's death in 1785 and was

Lebanon War Office on the evening of a paranormal investigation, circa 2015. *Photo by Martin J. Reardon Jr.*

not given proper care and restoration until it was commissioned to the care of the Connecticut Sons of the American Revolution in 1891.

When you visit the Lebanon War Office Museum, it doesn't take a vivid imagination to transport yourself back to the way things were in the eighteenth century and to feel as if you, too, may look over and see a man clad in a white wig, knickers just above the knee with long white socks, a long coat with tails and button vest, standing holding some sort of walking stick or sign of prominence among a table with others clad of similar distinguished service. You may hear the French accents of Lauzun and Rochambeau amid the old and proper English of Trumbull, Huntington or Williams as talk of supplies and movement to the Continental army take place. The meeting table is adorned with a few candles, with flames providing heat in the stone fireplace and the picturesque country green just out the window.

Colonial homes dot the street. The Trumbulls' grand home sits up the road, and the beaten path from Norwich to Hartford runs straight through the quaint village. Some may imagine that the Lebanon of 1775 may not vary much from its modern appearance. Its activity height was booming back then, so if anything it may just be a little quieter today. The ghosts of Lebanon's colorful past can still be found around the green and within the war office—whether it's a French soldier from Lauzun's army, a Continental army officer or Governor Trumbull himself, shadows are often reported walking about the war office.

Shamus Denniston of the Thames Society of Paranormal Investigations was the first to spend a dark night within the war office alongside his team in order to communicate with spirits of centuries past, and the activity captured all of their attention that evening in the early 2000s, with the image of a shadow moving through the old fireplace and coming out into the remainder of the war office. Strange, but perhaps the fireplace was a reminder of its past. I went along with my husband, my equipment and property steward Dave Packard from the Connecticut Sons of the American Revolution in the fall of 2015 to uncover exactly what spirits may abound. Utilizing an audio recorder, an SB7 Spirit Box and an EMF detector, we were prepared to encounter the spirits of Lebanon's past and hopefully some founding fathers. The EMF detector was oddly quiet for large parts of the three-hour investigation, until the mention of Governor Trumbull by Mr. Packard. We inquired if the spirits were familiar with Washington, Rochambeau or Huntington and heard small murmurs of male voices conversing over the audio devices as if they were talking to them. Mr. Packard asked if anyone knew Mr. Trumbull, and the murmurs continued; the EMF detector, having been unmoved up to that point, spiked up to illuminate all available colors. It was an affirmative yes, we inferred, and then the lights shut off. We had a follow-up question: "Are any of the aforementioned men present in the room at this time?" A distinct "yes" came through on the audio recorder and simultaneously on the spirit box in response as the room illuminated again.

Shadows captured the corner of our eyes from that moment on, and we were unable to debunk any as passing cars or other such sights. Proceeding to the second floor, there was an elusive feeling, a questioning feeling, not as grand as that of the spirits downstairs. Neighboring coyotes began to howl and cry outside as if in response to what was happening in the war office, and then we proceeded back downstairs as a group to the meeting room. Dave was dressed in his eighteenth-century reenactment best, and we thought to inquire of the spirits present if they liked his attire. Another clear "yes" indicated an affirmative response. We sat at the makeshift meeting table and inquired of various topics all the way from acquaintances to favorite drinks. Male voices abounded, shadows moved and the EMF detector took off once more but only at one chair at the table—a vacant one set apart from the three of us. Someone, it seemed, was sitting at that table with us, conversing. Whenever they spoke, the lights and audio responded. No imagination was needed—someone from the eighteenth century's military past was there. Perhaps someday devices will make it even better, to capture the details of what that man may have said to us, but his presence was distinct and made clear; he was there ready to plan something of great importance.

For a brief part of the investigation, we decided to speak French to entice any French soldiers buried around the war office. All was quiet except for the movement of shadows around the outside windows once more as the French language continued. Perhaps my French wasn't up to par, but it seemed to pique the curiosity of a passing spirit. Only twice has the war office been investigated and the volunteers reported nothing too frightening, but it is the most popular volunteer location belonging to the Connecticut Sons of the American Revolution. There's something about that location that people can't stay away from—a blend of history and spirit, letting us all know that it's still the most important place to be.

NORWICH

THE REBELLION'S BIRTHPLACE

LEFFINGWELL INN AND OLD NORWICHTOWN BURIAL GROUND

Leffingwell Inn, a notable tavern filled with the Patriots and rebels discussing the plans of their revolt, turned into a stronghold for war provisions much like the Lebanon War Office and housed some of the great Patriots of Connecticut's past, be them the Leffingwell family, who called this place home, or those of the visiting nature, who may have stayed here if only for a night.

Norwich in and of itself was home to Declaration of Independence signer Samuel Huntington and the Huntington family, as well as Benedict Arnold, the notorious brigadier general who fought on both sides of the war for undetermined reasons but became the most notable traitor who ever went down in American history. Norwich was the seventh-largest city in the colonies due to the location of it harboring an inland river, putting it right on the trade map. Ask any historian and they will tell you that waterways were the highways of the past, and if you had a waterway, your settlement became a beacon for trade and life. Trade in Norwich was primarily between New England and England and/or the West Indies.

It was this trade that put Benedict Arnold's family in Norwich. His father was in the mercantile business and became a man of great means, enrolling young Benedict in private school in Canterbury and intending for him to enroll at Yale when he was older. Arnold's family home was located nearly across the street from the Leffingwell's original location, and the tavern was a place frequented by his father, also named Benedict Arnold. A lesser-known fact is that young Benedict frequented the place as a boy and would be sent to retrieve his father from the tavern and, later, would find himself employed briefly as a young man by the Leffingwells within the tavern and by other town merchants to help support his family. Certainly, in a tavern like Leffingwell Inn, young Arnold would've been made privy to the very first talks among eastern Connecticut colonials of the new world they wanted to create.

A lifelong Norwich resident until his passing in 2010, Bill Stanley was an advocate for the colorful history of Benedict's Arnold's past and his reputation, and he educated thousands about Arnold's Norwich roots. Leffingwell House Museum is the only standing structure today that, while not directly related to the infamous Benedict Arnold family, houses the few remnants and belongings that remain today; it is devoted to the entire history of Norwich and the Revolutionary War era in Connecticut. Bill Stanley stated in an interview with a reporter from *Yankee Magazine* and the *New London Day* in 1999 that Leffingwell Tavern was actually the place where Benedict Arnold's father nearly drank himself to death after suffering deep depression when four of his six children died within a short time after

Leffingwell House Museum in Norwich, circa 2015. *Courtesy of the Society of the Founders of Norwich.*

contracting yellow fever. Benedict's father continued to drink, leading to a decrease in family money and family respect and leaving young Benedict unable to go to Yale; instead, he practiced as an apprentice with the Lathrop family—a successful apothecary and general trades merchant in Norwich.

Tragedy struck once and for all when Hannah Arnold, young Benedict's mother, passed in 1759 when he was just eighteen years old. Benedict and his mother were very close, and Benedict returned home to care for his father and young sister, as he had previously moved on to some ventures in New Haven. His father passed in 1761 after his history of public drunkenness and shame. Benedict Arnold was just a young man of twenty when his father passed and had dealt with the shame that had visited the family, as his father had been denied communion by the church due to his drunken behavior. Leffingwell was surely not to blame, as a tavern was a staple in any community of the eighteenth century; however, it did become the Arnold family drinking hole, to say the least. Young Benedict Arnold would go on later to sell the family homestead, and Norwich would become a thing of distant memory in his new life as a general in the war, in trade and so on.

Arnold's family home and birthplace was struck by lightning in October 1853; naturally, for some time, townsfolk did all they could to loot, steal or destroy anything thought to have belonged to the Arnold family. A bannister from the interior stairway was nearly all that was left of the Arnold family's homestead, birthplace of Benedict, and that piece of bannister is now at the Leffingwell House Museum. Hopeful excavators went to the Arnold family site in 1895 and were able to salvage one more thing of note. Ironically, this house stood on what is now referred to as Washington Street, but Arnold advocate Bill Stanley was able to ensure that the adjoining street would become Arnold Lane in his honor. Benedict Arnold's house key, which is now on display in a glass case in the Norwich history museum at the Leffingwell Inn Museum, was found at the site. It's the very same house key that Benedict Arnold kept in his pocket throughout the duration of the war, a dedication to his home in Norwich, according to Greg Farlow, president of the Society of the Founders of Norwich, which owns and operates the Leffingwell site.

The Arnold family pew from the church is another artifact. Each family had a pew assigned to them, and depending on their societal ranking, they would sit closer to the pulpit. The Arnold family pew was respectably close to the front and now sits in the tavern room of the Leffingwell Inn. If the ghost of Benedict Arnold is what you seek, he may still lurk around the halls of Leffingwell from time to time, around the few remaining items marking his childhood. Some believe that he may be felt across the street at the Norwichtown Burial Ground, where his mother's grave and his baby brother's grave lie, almost worn with age. Bill Stanley, in fact, used to hold events there on All Hallows' Eve with the townsfolk to see if he might pay them a visit. It's a stretch but certainly possible in a cemetery popularly regarded as the most haunted cemetery in the entire state of Connecticut.

It's true that Benedict Arnold may be the Revolutionary resident of Norwich who gained the most fame in history, but he was not by any stretch the man who made the most impact during the Revolution in Norwich. Samuel Huntington, Continental Congress president and Declaration signer, could give him a run for his money, but so could Colonel Christopher Leffingwell, friend of George Washington, proprietor, entrepreneur, Patriot and provisions provider, whose legacy is boasted at Leffingwell Inn Museum today. A frame house, the Leffingwell Homestead has the appearance of two saltbox houses put together over the years, and in a way, it was the combination of two houses during renovations and additions that formed the unique structure of the Leffingwell Inn.

Construction of the inn began in 1675, with numerous additions made prior to its completion just before the Revolution began in the 1770s. The interior and exterior structures encapsulate the late seventeenth- and early eighteenth-century eras in which they were built. Built in 1675, the tavern room, in particular, depicts the earliest stages of American Colonial architecture. (The tavern room was originally residential and was converted to a tavern in 1701 under the proprietorship of Thomas Leffingwell.) The land originally stood on a plot belonging to Stephen Backus, who was the founder of Norwich and acquired the property as all early settlers acquired their property, upon the settlement of the town in 1659. If you're a local, the Backus name is familiar—Backus Hospital is known throughout the eastern region, but not many may know who the namesake was.

The original building actually had its construction started via the Backus family rather than the Leffingwell family, as it was William Backus's son, Stephen, who began construction in 1675. This part of the building would be the southeast corner. The property transferred to Leffingwell hands in the year 1700, when Stephen Backus sold it to Thomas Leffingwell, and subsequently, he was granted permission to keep an inn on the property. It was tradition for many inns to also boast a tavern so that they could properly accommodate all of their guests' needs. Thomas Leffingwell was at the home for a few decades before he passed in 1724 and left the property to his son, Benajah Leffingwell, who continued to operate an inn and store. It was after his death that the Leffingwell Inn was inherited by the infamous Revolutionary War Patriot Colonel Christopher Leffingwell. Christopher completed the construction in the 1760s with additions to the north and older parts of the house.

After Christopher's eventual passing, the house went to his third wife and eventually ended up in the hands of his granddaughter, who was wife to Continental Congress delegate and U.S. House Representative of Connecticut Benjamin Huntington. From the nineteenth century onward, it remained in the Huntington family until 1943. In 1956, the property made its way to the Society of the Founders of Norwich, which has kept the property in a wonderful state and turned it into the historic museum for artifacts of the Leffingwells, Arnolds and all of Norwich during its time spent there. The property was moved adjacently across the street to its current position in the 1950s, as is depicted in one of the pictures in this chapter.

Beginning during Benajah's tavern-keeping days and throughout Christopher's, this was the very tavern where men would drink and complain about the government and begin to draft their first plans for colonial upheaval. Before anything was official, this tavern was a gathering place for Patriots and soon-to-be soldiers, as well as many Sons of Liberty. When you

Leffingwell Inn in Norwich during their mid-twentieth-century move, circa 1957–58. *Courtesy of the Society of the Founders of Norwich.*

Christopher Leffingwell Burial Site marker at Old Norwichtown Burial Ground in Norwich, circa 2016.

stand in the tavern room today, you can almost hear the discussion taking place among the clanking of glasses, the flames roaring in the fireplace, boot-stomping music and intense discussion among the hard workers and men of Norwichtown. Indeed, within the walls of this very tavern room, shadows are often seen walking about by the windows—so tall and military in bearing that you can't help but think that they are still meeting within that very room.

After Benajah's passing, revolutionary thought circled throughout colonies and at the inn. The *Report on Leffingwell Inn, Norwichtown, Connecticut* describes Colonel Leffingwell as an "enterprising and perspicacious business man, a pioneer in many fields." Indeed he was. His accomplishments include the establishment of the very first paper mill in Connecticut. There's a motivational saying that some in small business utilize today that would have also rung true for Leffingwell: "You spend a few years of your life living like most people won't so that you can spend the rest of your life living how most people can't."

This was true, as the paper mill was not at first an economic success, even though there was a financial need. Leffingwell even had to request government aid to lift the business off the ground and presented an argument to the government about the necessity of such a mill. The General Assembly of Connecticut Colony granted Leffingwell's request from 1769 to 1772 and provided the support the paper mill needed to succeed. Leffingwell's entrepreneurial spirit was not just confined to one venture. A true "Renaissance man," he also opened six additional factories and continued to operate the tavern. By the beginning of his wartime efforts, Christopher Leffingwell was the operator of eight businesses throughout the Norwich community, from paper to pottery and chocolate, as well as serving as innkeeper/tavern keeper, just to name a few.

As for the war, his patriotism was not hidden from the community, a Patriot stronghold by 1775, and he remained connected throughout the duration of the war. He led a company of light infantry, earning him the nickname "Colonel," and served as a confidential advisor to Governor Trumbull. His dedication resulted in his appointment to the Committee of Correspondence in 1775. This meant that his advisement would continue. As enemies approached port in New London, news would be delivered to Leffingwell, and his infantry would report to the area and defend accordingly. Leffingwell learned by communicating with Governor Trumbull and defending New London and Norwich, giving him expertise, and he was able to further advise in the securing of Fort Ticonderoga and in the engagement of Colonel Ethan Allen and the Green Mountain Boys in Vermont.

It wasn't long before General Washington learned what an asset Leffingwell was and began to develop a relationship. Washington frequently reached out for counsel and would visit Norwich and stay at the Leffingwell Tavern. While there, Leffingwell would supply Washington with provisions. Other than the Lebanon War Office, this was a favorite place for provisions and the other reason Connecticut came to be called the "Provision State" at the centennial. Washington noted that Connecticut had the best prices on goods and best supply of provisions, especially compared to Virginia, where Washington and the troops could rarely afford to receive supplies. Washington wasn't the only one looking to Leffingwell for provisions. Letters were also exchanged between Leffingwell and John Hancock regarding molasses and other goods. The Leffingwell family's ability to provide provisions was among the best in the nation. However, this ability was second only to Leffingwell's intelligence during the Revolutionary War. General Washington and Leffingwell were often able to discuss troop movement, defense plans and more. Leffingwell could identify weak spots in defense and let Washington know how they could be amended, and it is known that these discussions took place within the walls of the Leffingwell Inn during Washington's visits. Leffingwell honored the legacy of General Washington's visits by naming one of the rooms across the hall from the tavern room on the first floor "Washington's Room," perhaps the room in which he had accommodation for the night. It is adorned in Colonial décor, and pieces honor the late president throughout.

During an investigation held publicly with Seaside Shadows Tours and TAPS Home Team, I was able to take numerous guests to the Washington Room to investigate. Although quiet, there were significant temperature changes within the room that October evening. One of the guests inquired of any spirits present, "What's your name?" The spirit box seemingly responded, "George." Could it be true? Did Leffingwell leave such an impact with our former president? The guests and investigators had to be sure. Another guest inquired, "What is the name of your wife?" An indistinguishable name beginning with "M" came through the spirit box in response. Excitedly, we had hoped that it may indeed be Martha. That night, various team members and investigators saw a shadowy figure well over six feet tall walking in the adjacent tavern room and Washington Room. Sometimes it was bent over, as if inspecting the devices, and other times it was walking through. You could almost hear the boot steps. George Washington stood at six feet, two inches, remarkably tall for his time. This lends the hope that if a spirit shows up as it once was, perhaps Washington and Leffingwell still meet within the inn today.

Leffingwell's immense support did not go unnoticed when the nation was forged and separated from Britain at the close of the war. Due to his monitoring of Norwich and New London and all that he had done in the war as a defender in 1784, President Washington appointed Leffingwell as the new government's first naval officer. By 1789, changes were taking place, and his candidacy for collector's post was brought into question. The official port of entry for Connecticut was to be New Haven rather than Norwich. Humbly, Colonel Leffingwell wrote to Washington, "It is being suggested to me by worthy friend, Colonel Trumbull that General Huntington was one of my competitors for the office of Collector at the District of New

Leffingwell House Museum in Norwich, circa early 2000s. *Courtesy of the Society of the Founders of Norwich.*

London whose character is high in my estimation. Should your Excellency after comparing our claims qualifications and situation appoint him to the office, I earnestly solicit that may not be wholly unnoticed but be appointed Surveyor for the district."

Whether it was due to Washington's concerns for his age or influence of others, Mr. Leffingwell did not receive appointment as surveyor or collector in 1789. Jedediah Huntington was named to the collector's post, and Mr. Nathaniel Richards was appointed surveyor. This did not diminish Leffingwell's legacy by any stretch; rather, it gave him an opportunity to continue operating the inn and mills, as well as live his life with his family. Christopher Leffingwell continued in service to his country, to Connecticut and to Norwich until his death at home in 1810 at the age of seventy-six.

Spirit activity abounds throughout the Leffingwell Museum. As I took a tour with museum archivist Richard Guidebeck, activity seemed to peak around us as we talked of all things history. In the Washington Room, I was instructed not to touch anything and just to look—a rule common in many museums. I tenderly walked through the room, admiring its adornments, and left with Richard by my side. About twenty minutes later, Society of the Founders of Norwich president Greg Farlow and his wife, Cam, arrived. Cam immediately walked into the Washington Room and inquired, "Who knocked over these frames?" pointing at the picture frames on the desk that had fallen. I had seen them standing up and hadn't heard a sound. She picked them up, and we laughed, "Maybe they're letting us know they're around." Cam and Greg continued to be gracious hosts and then took off for the day, leaving me once more with Richard, the man who knows all things Norwich and Leffingwell Inn down to the last detail. He kindly took me to the archives to show me all the documentation and artifacts that remain in the basement. As we sat by his library computer, we heard the door upstairs open and footsteps come in. It was strange, as the door had been locked after the Farlows' exit, and it was the off-season, so no visitors could just waltz in. Richard, of course, ran upstairs to determine what or who it was. I heard him say, "Hello? Is anyone there?" I heard only silence in response. Richard came back quietly and resumed our discussion as normal. I had to ask, "What happened up there, Richard?" "Oh, it was nothing," he replied. I couldn't help but smirk, thinking, "Wow, it's them; they can't help but walk around when they have visitors and host them as well."

During the public investigation with Seaside Shadows and TAPS Home Team, a variety of experiences occurred, as guests and investigators made contact with spirits from the eighteenth, nineteenth and early twentieth

Above: Old Norwichtown Burial Ground by Cemetery Road entrance in Norwich, circa 2016.

Left: Burial place of Hannah Arnold, mother of Benedict Arnold, at Old Norwichtown Burial Ground in Norwich, circa 2016.

centuries. Audible sounds, shadow figures, ghostly feelings and more abounded. The basement, which housed Revolutionary muskets, cannons, portraits and more alongside Civil War–era artifacts, seemed to be a hotbed for activity. Electromagnetic fields fluctuated despite no electronics being present, and the spirit box had male voices speak of cannons and portraits, as if leading guests to the artifacts within the walls that were theirs.

Leffingwell is filled with letters, belongings, toys, clothing, weapons, tools and more of Norwich's fascinating past, and it is a worthwhile visit for both the paranormal and history buff. If you are looking for something more ghostly on your Norwich stroll, just down the road and across the way is one of the oldest and most historic cemeteries in the state: Norwichtown Burial Ground. There you can find the graves of Christopher Leffingwell, Hannah Arnold, Samuel Huntington (the Declaration signer) and more. Numerous Leffingwells were buried here, as were Huntingtons, some of the largest and most influential family names of the American Revolution. The stone belonging to Arnold's mother and brother who died in infancy is almost worn away, and stones around it are broken or removed. Looters and such

Burial place of Samuel Huntington, Declaration signer and Continental Congress president, at Old Norwichtown Burial Ground in Norwich, circa 2016.

Old Norwichtown Cemetery memorial dedicated to twenty Revolutionary French soldiers who died in camp at Norwichtown, photograph circa 2015. *Photo by Martin J. Reardon Jr.*

Old Norwichtown Burial Ground bridge and entrance to additional grounds in Norwich, circa 2016.

weren't always kind to Arnold family memory, but the presence is clear, and a small plaque marks the site where young Benedict Arnold once stood at a family burial—a place where you, too, can stand.

Samuel Huntington has an extravagant display that was built posthumously, paying homage to his service and to the Declaration of Independence. His original burial site, much smaller and humbler, lies right beside it. The Daughters of the American Revolution Faith Trumbull Chapter had dedicated a memorial to General Lafayette, a French hero and supporter of the Americans during the Revolution who along with the Continental army dedicated their lives to the cause of American independence. Wintering was hard, however, as the climate was harsh and conditions not sustainable in Connecticut. The monument is dedicated to the twenty soldiers who passed away in Norwich during such conditions and reads as follows: "In Memory of Twenty French Soldiers Who, Serving under Lafayette, Died While in Camp at Norwich Town 1778." Twenty French flags are kept in their honor, surrounding the memorial.

Norwichtown Burial Site is a haunting site, although a main road passes by it with a McDonald's, a Bank of America and other commercial enterprises. Just up the cemetery road, there is a quiet calmness, where the sound dissipates and you see a burial ground as it once was—a Norwich as it once stood. Spiritualists and sensitives alike throughout the state will often remark that this is the most profound place of spirit activity they've ever encountered. Upon arrival, the spirits of soldiers and others can be seen rising up and paying their respects to the visitor, saying hello. It's as if walking through a crowded yet quiet township all its own. Pictures are taken by guests showing things they can't quite explain—mists and faces, yet all of them smiling, proud to look at the America they helped to build. If ever there was a cemetery to pay respect to your founding fathers, Connecticut houses at least two—Norwichtown Burial Ground is one of them.

Norwich, the seventh-largest city of the colonies, was home of Benedict Arnold, Samuel Huntington and Christopher Leffingwell and host to George Washington; today it harbors eighteenth-century spirits.

September 6, 1781

The Burning of New London and the Battle at Groton Heights

Fort Griswold and Ye Antientist Burial Ground

September 6, 1781, is a date that lives on throughout the Nutmeg State. It is the day that Norwich, Connecticut's own Benedict Arnold—newly turned Loyalist—set his sights painfully close to home to neighboring cities Groton and New London, Connecticut. The landscape he would attack sits a mere twenty miles from his hometown of Norwich. Commander Arnold, with his new Tory allies, would face the men he once fought alongside, the neighbors he once lived among, and burn their homes to the ground and fight them to the death at Fort Griswold. New London was a safe harbor, a home for many privateer ships that were enemies to the British Regulars. Some would consider them pirates with a license. Stores throughout New London housed anything these privateers might need for battle. The British also knew that it was the fault of these New Londoners that the merchant ship *Hannah*, which carried supplies from New York, ended up being captured. They wanted revenge for this. September 6, 1781, the day of the Burning of New London and the Battle of Groton Heights, forever changed the landscape of southeastern Connecticut and the dynamic between Arnold and his home territory.

Only a single night's notice was provided from Patriot spy David Gray, who delivered Colonel Ledyard news of an impending attack. His report to Colonel Ledyard in the late evening of September 5 noted that Arnold would be arriving to attack New London with a large navy. He was last seen approaching New London from Huntington Harbor. The worried yet motivated spy suggested calling militias from surrounding towns. It seemed, however, that time was working against them to make the plea to anyone else, and for the most part, New London was on its own. New London's own hero, naval admiral Nathaniel Shaw, was not present, having set out with a small hunting party heading east along the coast, clearly not anticipating a large-scale attack. One of its largest assets being out of town left New London on its own and with limited resources.

Governor Trumbull received the news late on September 5 as well, but this message of warning was from General Washington, who reported that he feared a "hostile attack upon or invasion of this state"—this state, of course, being Connecticut. Plans began to take place immediately, but it was too little, too late. Washington had received news of a French fleet arriving in the Chesapeake and reported there to bring support alongside Rochambeau. In New London, they all made an effort to remove some valuable assets and prepare for defense as best they could in the hours they had. However, as nightfall arrived, Arnold and his fleet made their way from Long Island. By three o'clock in the morning, just as the sun began to rise, the British ships were spotted by a man on duty at Fort Griswold in Groton.

Fort Griswold had just reached the completion of its structure. Construction of the immense fortification began soon after the Battles of Lexington and Concord in 1775. The original lower battery was completed quickly, but the upper fort was not completed until 1779. The man on duty, Mr. Avery, immediately called for the support of his captain, William Latham, who arrived promptly, and the pair of them loaded two large cannons and began to fire them off, sounding the alarm of enemy arrival. Benedict Arnold heard and responded with a play on what was then common knowledge: three cannons firing, signaling good news or, at least, no news. Knowing this, when Avery and Latham requested help with two firings, Arnold set off a third firing—telling people essentially that all was well.

Colonel Ledyard knew better. He had received the news the night before and knew that Arnold's arrival was imminent. Ledyard summoned for help, but it proved difficult to convince men that it wasn't a false alarm due to the three cannon firings. Some from neighboring towns began to see smoke rise in New London as burning commenced and made their way to assist as hastily as humanly possible. The Hempstead men who lived not far from the Shaw Mansion awoke and prepared for battle. Stephen Hempstead made his way to Fort Trumbull, and his cousin John made his way to the city.

Admiral Nathaniel Shaw watched helplessly by Fisher's Island as the enemy fleet blocked his way home. It was a sobering reminder to Colonel Ledyard that he alone would have to lead the defense. Ledyard and those he could convince to rise up and fight made their way to Groton and Fort Griswold. His parting words as he boarded the ferry were, "If I must lose honor or life today you who know me best can tell which it will be."

In the city of New London, Benedict Arnold arrived with his Thirty-eighth Regiment of "Loyal Americans." In all, 1,600 Loyalists arrived on the shores of New London and Groton. Four companies of the regiment headed to Fort Trumbull and subsequently Fort Griswold. The rest followed Arnold into the city. The Americans were outnumbered by Loyalists about ten to one. Due to this extreme difference, one hundred volunteers reporting under Captain Nathaniel Saltonstall obeyed his orders to divide into two groups and create a distraction of sorts rather than engage in direct combat. Saltonstall felt that this was their best bet. They hosted a running firefight and carried away wounded. General Arnold brought his troops into town to commence the burning—his targets were any locations that were stockpiles of goods or naval stores. (Although he was discernably wise, Arnold presumably didn't realize something: gunpowder was in one of the stockpiles and would be set ablaze, and when ignited, it would be a large explosion and take down all the buildings surrounding it.)

Arnold's men continued despite the sporadic firing from Saltonstall's men. One of Arnold's major targets other than the Hempstead family strongholds was, of course, the notable Shaw Mansion, where only Nathaniel's beautiful wife, Lucretia, and their servants were available to salvage anything. It was indeed the Shaw Mansion that Arnold went for first, knowing that it was Shaw's privateers who had taken the ship *Hannah*. It's important to note that Arnold was acting under orders simply to retrieve the *Hannah*, not to set fire and begin battle. It would seem that Arnold went on a bit of a rogue mission on September 6. Arnold and his men burned down the captured *Hannah* drifting at the end of Shaw's dock and set fire to Shaw's office and storehouse in a separate structure on the property near to the stone house.

Lucretia was able to salvage many books and papers; however, the chest containing Connecticut's naval office papers perished. The Hempsteads also hid their family papers. Many of the Hempsteads and other volunteers were around the city hiding and defending where they could. Some volunteers were able to fire cannons at approaching redcoats, but to limited success. The city was surrounded by Arnold and his men, and fires were started

Portrait of Benedict Arnold as painted by John Trumbull and copyrighted by Ed Frossard, circa 1894. *Courtesy of the Library of Congress.*

nearly everywhere, whether it was a warehouse, shipping stronghold or a family homestead such as Captain Saltonstall's house. Stephen Hempstead's house was destroyed, leaving his family fleeing for miles into the forest. It remains unknown to this day if some of these fires were truly accidents from setting fire to a large amount of gunpowder or if Arnold gave the orders to set these homes ablaze on purpose.

One particular household encounter during all of this remains unique, and it is the story of a brave woman named Abigail Hinman who took to defending her own home against her former friend and neighbor, Benedict Arnold. Abigail did not evacuate her house. She had known Arnold from her time living in Norwich and hosting him at her dinner table. She witnessed the arrival of his men, and Arnold even approached her home, graciously saluted her and promised her safety. She and her home would be spared. Hinman wasn't fooled by this seeming act of kindness but would take advantage of any favors he might be willing to spare. To save her neighbors' homes, she claimed that her husband owned their properties and gained them protection. Arnold obliged and carried forward. Hinman watched from her rooftop, and as Arnold began to depart, her outrage at this man, this friend turned traitor, overwhelmed her. Holding her musket, she fired it at General Arnold directly. *Boom! Snap!* The sound penetrated the air, but lo and behold, it was a misfire, one that General Arnold heard. She quickly dropped the musket out of sight as Arnold whipped around to inquire about the sound. Despite the suspicion on his face, she claimed that it was a breaking piece of furniture. He nodded in understanding and took off into New London, never truly knowing of Abigail Hinman's near success in taking him down, this most notorious traitor in American history.

The chaos of the burning had opened up a storehouse filled with the *Hannah*'s treasures, and it was completely looted by Loyalists and possibly criminals with no particular allegiance to either side. Traitors and friends of Arnold's were seemingly everywhere, their identities kept secret as Arnold's men burned down their houses as well to keep suspicion at bay. These men could be considered to be the access points that made this ruin of New London possible.

By the end of the burning of the city alone, not the battle, twelve American ships that were stuck in the harbor were burned, along with thirty-seven dock storefronts, fifty cannons, the battery, wharves, the printing office, the mill, the customhouse, eighteen town shops, twenty barns, the jail and, last but not least, sixty-five homesteads. In late eighteenth-century New England, cities were remarkably small. Not much of New London city was able to survive this horrendous day.

As eight hundred British Regulars rampaged New London, burning down seemingly everything in sight, across the river in Fort Griswold, Groton, a forty-five-minute battle ensued, turning into one of the bloodiest Revolutionary War battles to take place. No available weapon was left unused during this battle—muskets, bayonets, swords, pikes and even cannons,

Left: Portrait of Abigail Hinman protecting her home during the 1781 New London burning, painted by Daniel Huntington, circa 1854. *Courtesy of New London Landmarks.*

Below: Sketch of Fort Griswold in Groton, circa 1836. *Courtesy of Wikipedia.*

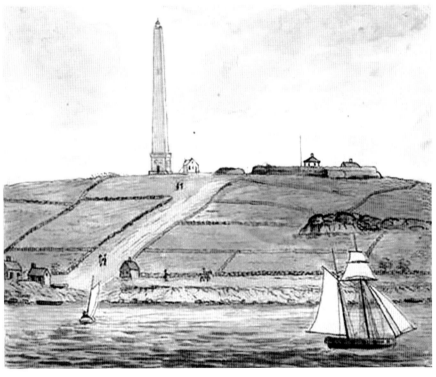

which were literally thrown over the walls onto the British side by a man named Samuel Edgecomb Jr. Erich Lehman wrote of this fatal battle at Fort Griswold in *Homegrown Terror*, stating, "The Battle at Groton Heights was the bloodiest battle of the entire war with the highest percentage of soldiers participating killed. And almost all the Americans had been killed after the surrender. New London suffered the highest percentage of destruction of any American city."

The timing was complicated. As the city was going up in flames, the British first made their way toward Fort Trumbull of New London, directly across from Fort Griswold. Having most of the men already summoned to Fort Griswold, only 23 remained at Fort Trumbull, including Stephen Hempstead and his family. They fired a single volley, spiked the guns and hastily took off to Fort Griswold trying to escape capture. Captain Shapley led the efforts at Fort Trumbull in New London under Colonel Ledyard's command. The men put up a valiant defense, but Fort Trumbull was taken with ease by the British; 7 of Shapley's men were injured and one of their vessels taken. However, they were also able to take down 4 or 5 of Arnold's men, who then set their sights across the Thames River on Fort Griswold, where Ledyard stood with about 160 to 180 brave men who were ready to take on the 800 British Loyalists arriving under the leadership of Lieutenant Eyre. Although the rebels were but an ensemble of militiamen with no experience, volunteers with no training and numerous children, outnumbered about 6 to 1, their motivation was pure and the purpose that filled their bodies and minds was intense and fierce. These men also believed that 200 to 300 more militiamen from surrounding areas would soon arrive and be able to assist. Based on this, Ledyard's small war council believed that the odds might well turn to their favor and adamantly and finally refused to surrender.

About 150 buildings erupted in flames in New London as the Battle at Fort Griswold was set to commence. Some of the men were delayed on their voyage up the river by natural conditions, but soon the remaining hundreds of Loyalists from New York and New Jersey arrived and the bloody battle began. According to accounts from a twelve-year-old watch boy, the regiments landed between 10:30 a.m. and 11:00 a.m. at Fort Griswold. The British sent Captain Beckwith with a flag first and foremost demanding that the men of Fort Griswold surrender upon their arrival. Colonel Ledyard sent back the early American flag accompanied with the fateful message that he would "maintain the fort to the last extremity."

The British responded once more with a parley flag with the message that they would show no mercy if they did not surrender. While men around

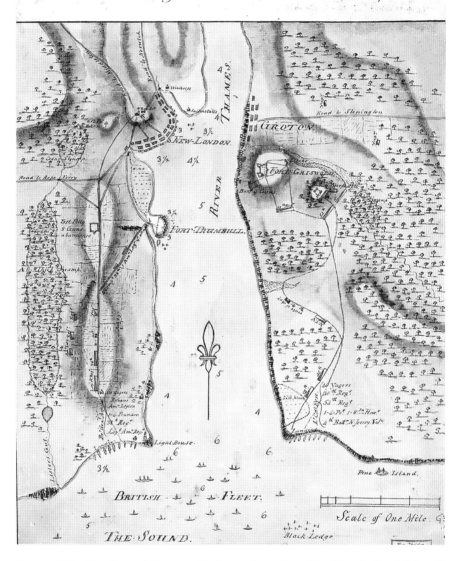

A map of New London and Groton, with the attacks made on Forts Trumbull and Griswold in the 1781 Battle at Groton Heights. *Courtesy of Wikipedia.*

him argued what was best, with calm and purposeful mind Colonel Ledyard repeated his statement that he would "maintain the fort to the last extremity."

Cannonballs were hurled over forcefully, yet unsuccessfully, from the conquered Fort Trumbull directly at Groton Height's Fort Griswold. Those men at Fort Griswold, knowing the terrain and equipment better, returned cannonball fire with more success. The battle was officially underway. Not just the Thirty-eighth regiment but also the Fortieth and Fifty-fourth Regiments were available. Most of the Thirty-eighth stayed at Fort Trumbull, while Eyre led the Fortieth and Fifty-fourth into Fort Griswold. They met a small, rapid-fire defense as they came into the northeast corner but quickly overtook them, causing the defenders to flee to the larger part of the fort. Ledyard successfully fired cannons at the approaching soldiers, who were firing their muskets relentlessly, taking down twenty of the enemy British immediately. The rest scattered. As more British tried to charge at the unrelenting Americans, they continued with their musket fire and cannons, taking down British Regulars left and right, including their commanding officer, Eyre. Their groans of agony and moans of death could be heard all around the field. The men lay there writhing in pain and dying in multiple failed attempts to take over this ragged crew of volunteers fighting for their freedom. Was this to be a success after all? Had Fort Griswold truly provided protection for them?

It was not over yet. Due to an American flag being cut through by bullets, the British misinterpreted it as surrender. With joyful anticipation, they charged at the fort a fourth time, and the motley crew of Ledyard's men was ready, definitely not retreating. The indomitable Samuel Edgecomb hoisted cannonballs at them, even throwing them down onto the British. They fired relentlessly and then utilized even more weaponry—spears and sharp pikes—to keep the British at bay. British officers were successfully stabbed, but the Americans wouldn't remain untouched, either. Stephen Hempstead—who would leave this battle bloody and beaten and was even thought dead—received his first wound while firing a cannon. A musket ball grazed his head, causing him to gush blood over the fort. Bandaging it quickly with a piece of cloth, Hempstead remained unhalted and grabbed a pike, ready to fight. Another piece of enemy ammunition struck Hempstead in the arm, but he remained unhalted and picked himself back up; the Americans continued to fight off the attacking Loyalists. Most of the Americans were kin to one another. As the battle got bloodier, father, son and grandson watched one another perish in front of their very eyes but courageously continued on.

The ragtag team of Americans saw quite a bit of success. The more the redcoats arrived, the more they were able to disarm and kill them. Of the 160 to 180 defenders, only 10 were lost and a small number injured. Ledyard felt, however, that without reinforcements, the time had come to surrender. They could not keep it up much longer. Ledyard ordered the ceasefire, but perhaps this was one of those instances that bred the saying, "All is fair in love and war." All things are possible, and sometimes even surrender isn't honored. Ledyard's surrender at Fort Griswold was his fateful last act. Ledyard met the swarming British, surrendered and even handed the enemy his sword. The enemy's response was to take Colonel Ledyard's sword and swiftly run it through his body.

It seemed that this was the beginning of the end. Erratic behavior and violence seemed fair and took place indiscriminately. Ledyard's kin, like so many others, saw horrendous murder—the site is marked with this intense energy even today. His nephews charged at the British but were taken down. Others rushed them but also met their fates. The British were everywhere. Stephen Hempstead, as if not injured enough already, was stabbed in the hip, a wound that would give him a debilitating limp for the rest of his life. Many other Americans were shot, stabbed and left with their fatal and nonfatal wounds alike lying all over Fort Griswold in the skirmish. Nearly entire families were killed, leaving only widows, daughters and sisters who hopefully survived the tragic burnings taking place in New London. It was chaos. Some lay there begging, and if they were lucky and had anything of value, they might have been able to bribe a British officer not to kill them. Such is the story of Charles Eldredge, who was wounded in the knee and bought his life with his gold watch. Some American rebels were running away where they could, but the number of defenders dead now vastly outstripped the number of enemy dead.

The ammunition magazine and barracks provided shelter for many wounded. These 1700s structures disintegrated and fell years ago—only nineteenth-century structures remain at the site today. However, the intense energy of the wounded gathering, wishing for help, can still be felt and almost heard in the whispers of the wind today. Some British soldiers did fire into the safe hold for the wounded, until a commanding officer berated them for doing so. He made it clear that there was a line between battle and maliciousness—killing the wounded, who weren't fighting any longer, would do no good. After all, they were all human and shared that, even if they were on vastly different sides of the conflict.

Fort Griswold fortification and American flag, Groton, circa 2015. *Photo by Shelby McInvale.*

The battle had, for all intents and purposes, ended with a Loyalist victory over the rebels, but the torture and pain would continue. As many as 88 colonial soldiers and 51 British soldiers lay dead, with at least 36 colonials wounded (many mortally and would die later). Although the British death toll was significantly less, they had 135 wounded, nearly a quarter of the men who fought—all this from a group of men outnumbered 6 to 1, some would say. As the wounded lay among the dead across Fort Griswold, the British job was not done. The Regulars stripped many the dead and wounded, taking any valuable assets and weapons they could find on them. The dying, wounded rebels were corralled together and promised execution come morning.

As the surviving members of the Fortieth and Fifty-fourth Regiments gathered the wounded, they forced them into the town and threw the crippled into a cart. Stephen Hempstead was in one of these ammunition carts that was dealt with haphazardly and sent crashing into a tree stump. There was no regard for the barely breathing life that was left in these men and boys. The British buried their dead in a ditch at the fort, where their bodies remain to this day. The American dead were left where they fell or put in a wheelbarrow and thrown off the cliff. Many of the bodies were recovered and later taken and buried in local graveyards; many ended up in the Starr Burying Ground of Groton. Still others, even some locals, were left where they fell for all eternity. Blood-soaked and body-covered land is exactly what Fort Griswold became in its inaugural years.

What about all those survivors? The directionally challenged New Jersey Loyalists had finally made their way to the fray and assisted in burning the town and taking prisoners from the battlefield and beyond back to the ships. Some, such as the Ledyard family men who survived, were able to convince the British to parole them and their fellow badly wounded men—thirty-five in total. They were then brought to the ground floor of the house of one of their fellow wounded, Ebenezer Avery, including Stephen Hempstead. Other rebels were taken on board the warships as prisoners to New York; about twenty-eight men saw this fate. Some died aboard the ships or in the hazardous conditions to which they were exposed. Others were released. Ebenezer Ledyard, in a true act of martyrdom, was taken hostage for the men on parole. A twelve-year-old wounded boy, William Latham, was also subsequently released. The Avery House was one of the only homes left standing, as the British also took to burning down what was then the small town of Groton, leaving very little behind.

Fort Griswold monument view, Groton, circa 2015. *Photo by Shelby McInvale.*

Citizens and allies of the rebels and Ledyard in Colchester and Lebanon, Connecticut, were able to send assistance. Declaration signer William Williams, the son-in-law of Trumbull of Lebanon, rode mightily and swiftly, arriving in New London just as the town sat in ashes and Arnold and his men were seen sailing away. Meanwhile, at Fort Griswold, an effort to identify the wounded and the dead was taking place. Major Nathan Peters entered and immediately saw a fire spreading to the gunpowder magazine. He quickly snuffed it out, saving the entire area from an explosion of unknown size. Widows came from all over the area to look at the mutilated, bloodied and barely recognizable dead and wounded strewn across the field and at the Avery House. Other female family members took this time to come to the rescue, including Miss Fanny Ledyard, the niece of Colonel Ledyard. Not knowing her uncle's fate, she bravely arrived at the Avery House and tended immediately to a man wounded beyond recognition, with dirt and blood covering his skin. Her feet were soon covered in blood as well. She tended to his wounds and served him hot chocolate. This was an act the gentleman, Stephen Hempstead, would remember for life. It wasn't until later that she was informed of her uncle's death.

Another notable female figure was someone affectionately called "Mother Bailey," also known as Anna Warner Bailey. She was only twenty-two years old when the Battle at Groton Heights began. Her uncle, local farmer Edward Mills, with whom she lived after her parents' passing, proceeded to the battle site. Anna proclaimed her disdain for the Tories and a longing to fight, but a woman couldn't fight in the traditional sense in those days. That didn't stop her from doing what she could. When Edward went to fight at Fort Griswold, he left behind his wife, a young boy and an infant. The family waited anxiously and expectantly for news of his well-being or, better yet, his arrival, as they watched the smoke rise and heard the gunfire persist. The gunfire eventually ceased, and they heard no news. Nightfall came, and Edward did not return home from the deadly battlegrounds. They began to fear the worst, but Anna was determined to find her uncle, this man who had taken her in, and reunite him with his family.

Barefoot, Anna began a three-mile hike at dawn down the lane now known as 184, past all the worried relatives who surrounded the streets. She arrived at the makeshift hospital at the Avery House and found her uncle suffering the slow and painful death of exsanguination. He gave his niece one final request, wishing to see his family and say goodbye. Anna hurried back to the farm, saddled the horse and gathered the family; she carried the baby all the way until they arrived. She placed the infant in the arms of her dying Patriot uncle as she watched the dear family say goodbye.

Anna's rage at the British grew. She married a Fort Griswold survivor, Elijah Bailey, two years later in 1783. The couple became innkeepers famous for their outspoken views on American independence, and when the War of 1812 later took off, her denunciation of the Brits became famous. Their inn was a safe harbor for all those who felt the same. Her legacy was inspired in part by that of her dear uncle, who gave his life in the Battle of Groton Heights, framing her as one of the most formidable women to have lived in Revolutionary-era Connecticut.

Inside the Avery House, the makeshift hospital was filled with indescribable horror and the wounded. The energy is still palpable at the Ebenezer Avery House in Groton today, where it was moved closer to Fort Griswold in an effort to save the building in the 1970s. Its new location is now much closer to the battle site. In a piece published just this past October in the *New London Day*, staff writer Jessica Hopper interviewed the director of the nearby Groton Avery-Copp Museum regarding haunted history surrounding the homestead as well. The director, Leslie Evans, confirmed that many neighbors have witnessed phantom images of people in the windows walking around the house in the dead of night or on a weekend day, when the establishment is closed to all visitors or employees. Employees report the sounds of footsteps on vacant floors and the feeling of others knowing they were there—all innocent, perhaps, but the energy is distinct.

The legacy of all those passed too soon was carried on for many years by a man who was, at the time of the battle, only a fourteen-year-old boy named Jonathan Brooks. He witnessed the attack on New London and is to thank for much of the documentation we have on this day. Jonathan Brooks went to the fort on the anniversary of the battle every year, without fail, to tell the story of that day in grand detail and to pay honor to those who fell. No matter the weather or conditions, he would never miss a September 6 until he died. It is reported that one year the weather was so frightful that no one could attend, but Brooks wasn't stopped. He stood at the hillside fort and proclaimed loudly, "Attention, universe!" He proceeded to recount the whole story as he always had. Believe it or not, he was also at one time a presidential candidate for the United States. A unique man, indeed.

On September 6, 1781, Groton Heights, Fort Griswold, was drowned in the tears of widows, daughters and mothers as their loved ones—husbands, brothers and sons—lay lifeless in front of them. Some were just mere boys and others grown men who fought to the death for a cause they believed in with their whole hearts. In the ditch nearby, a pile of bloodied redcoats lay—they, too, lay dead, having participated in a massacre for which they felt their king would be proud.

It seems that these men continue to wage war, fight for freedom and let others know what happened to them; perhaps they search for the answers as to what exactly happened to them that early fall morning. Both local residents and paranormal investigators alike have been drawn to the impenetrable fort for years, trying to grasp the enormity of the history that occurred there. One team, the Paranormal Research Society of New England (PRSNE), founded by TV's "Haunted Collector," John Zaffis, found itself investigating the old fort in the early 2000s. On the day PRSNE arrived, investigators Carlos Reis, Dan LeRoy and Dominick Onofrio entered the stone tunnel leading toward the trench where much of the battle took place and where many British approached from. Midway through the tunnels, all of the investigators stopped in their tracks silently yet simultaneously. They all felt it—a heaviness in the air that you could cut with a knife. The wind whipped around them outside, but inside the tunnel, the air was heavy, unmoving, and the energy was intense. The three men stood there for twenty minutes trying to place what kind of energy this would be. They narrowed down a spot where the shift in energy seemed to be pulsating. Carlos stated that the spot was about two feet from the ground level up into the wall. An EVP session to conduct audio dialogue with the spirits was put on hold, and Carlos placed his recorder on a nearby ledge. The men proceeded into the fort, leaving the remarkable intensity they had experienced behind them—all of them in agreement that they experienced this together but none able to identify what it was.

They progressed onward to conduct EVP sessions in other sections of the fort. Dan Leroy had his recorder at the ready, pointed toward where the cannons are placed, facing toward the area of Fort Trumbull. Before the session took place, the investigators had gathered together to discuss what exactly they wanted to inquire of the soldiers. As they spoke to one another, a voice they did not recognize chimed in, as if to contribute to the conversation and the game plan. They each looked at one another in joint realization that none of them had just spoken the words they heard. That was clearly another man, but it seemed jumbled, mumbled. The voice was indeed captured on that recorder, but what he said remains indiscernible to this day. Was a soldier trying to get his story in there? Perhaps request a

Right: Fort Griswold casualty and wounded dedication plaque, Groton, circa 2015. *Photo by Shelby McInvale.*

Below: Fort Griswold stone tunnel view, Groton, circa 2015. *Photo by Shelby McInvale.*

conversation? It is hard to say, but it could be this very man that appeared as a full-bodied apparition later that night to Dan.

As they looked up to the entrance nearer the side where Colonel Ledyard met his demise, slain by his own sword, they saw the steep embankment that ran over the aforementioned tunnel. Standing on that lonely embankment was a man clear as day—the color of his clothes did not appear red, so a Patriot, perhaps? He held a musket in his hand and wore a tricorn hat. He briefly looked back at Mr. LeRoy and vanished moments later. Cold spots abounded and were reported by both Carlos and Dan. They did what any seasoned investigator would do and tried to measure these cold spots with their thermometer, which repeatedly malfunctioned throughout the night. Coincidence? Not likely. All sorts of equipment, from cameras to recorders and thermometers, is thought to malfunction when spirit energy is nearby—perhaps it manipulates the devices to give itself a boost. The exact reason is a mystery, but it repeatedly happens in the most spiritual of spots.

The PRSNE crew had plenty of experiences that night. Upon arriving home, Carlos realized an unfortunate fact: he had left his EVP recorder on that ledge while experiencing that intense energy. Ah well, he thought. Later, seemingly unexpected, he found himself in the Groton area for a soccer game, and Fort Griswold was not a far jump. "I have to go back," he thought. It seemed fate, after all, for Carlos. He pulled up to Fort Griswold, and the wind whipped around him as never before. As he exited his vehicle and proceeded into the fort, the phantom smell of gunpowder filled the air. He couldn't believe its intense odor. He looked around—had reenactors just been here? The flag was at half-staff. Had there been a salute? It was a sunny Saturday at noon. He looked around, but not a soul was in sight. He looked across the river and saw no activities and heard no events. What was that smell? It seemed to have lingered from the battle, the energy still entrenched in the earth.

As an author, paranormal business owner and spirit medium, I am often called on to investigate haunted sites, and by mere habit I bring with me an audio recorder at all times. I arrived on a beautiful late spring day in 2014 and was stunned by Fort Griswold. Accompanied by a few teammates, the wind whipped around us violently, a reminder of all the battering that had once taken place on the ground where we stood. We walked into that same tunnel toward the trench, having not spoken to Carlos and the PRSNE team at all by this point. As we went into that tunnel, that same energy engulfed us, a staleness as the wind whipped the flag against the pole outside. There was a longing, something missing, a story to be told. For a split second, we could all envision an injured man lying on the ground of that tunnel, gasping for air and waiting for one last message to be delivered. Perhaps he placed a letter to be delivered that was covered throughout the years? Whatever his message, we could not hear the audio that day because of the whipping winds. But his legacy, his energy, lives in that tunnel, and perhaps someday we will find what message this soldier needed delivered.

You do not need to be an investigator to experience the Battle at Groton Heights. History buffs, enthusiasts or curious visitors alike may experience the soul-filled history that Fort Griswold provides. Evan J. Andripoulos, local resident, town historian and historic home owner closely associated with New London Landmarks, has ventured to the fort with his family on numerous occasions. It is now a pleasant state park, perfect for picnics, small walks and a nice game of Frisbee. Evan, a connoisseur of all things local history, wanted to explore a bit more during one of his visits a few years back in the mid-2000s. He had recently heard that you could put a ghost finder application of some sort on your mobile phone. He had downloaded it previously and tried it out, but despite *USA Today*'s recommendation, it had limited success—until he and his loved ones arrived at Fort Griswold. Evan and his sons approached the spot where Colonel Ledyard fell and decided to utilize the app one more time. As they turned it on, they sensed orbs moving around them, and the detector indicated this as well. Numbers indicating electromagnetic field detections and more increased dramatically in the application. As goose bumps covered the arms of Evan and his two boys, they bravely turned on the audio. The application will tell you words that the spirits may be saying: "Consequences, Final Measure, STOP!" Evan's wife was there, too, a self-described skeptic, and she immediately felt sickness overcome her. They all decided that it was time to leave. They had just delved into that spirit realm a little too far.

Flash-forward a few years later, and Evan and his boys were once again frequenting the fort, this time in the winter of 2014–15 during a sledding trip. When they arrived, they found themselves in the company of a handful of other sledders. After a fun-filled day of sledding, one of Evan's boys inquired, "Can we use that app again?" Hesitantly, Evan obliged. It immediately pinged, indicating the presence of surrounding spirits. Evan talked to the surrounding ghosts, "Show me a sign that you are near us," and within a second of this request, a single hair of blondish color floated on the wind and landed on his son's arm. They looked back to the handful of people around them and were astonished to find that they all had dark hair. It hadn't come from one of them. Again, they put this story in their memory as another event at Fort Griswold reminding them that their history lives on and that the brave men who lost their lives there continue to march through the trenches, fight for the freedom of those around them and protect all they held dear.

Remember the cart filled with the injured, such as Stephen Hempstead, not all of whom survived, especially after being pushed down a hill in the cart and into a tree stump? It is thought to be one of the most traumatic events of September 6, 1781, leaving behind one of the deepest spiritual scars. As the cart crashed, the cries, moans and yells of agony could be heard across the river into New London. As Jessica Hopper reported in her segment, even today, local residents claim to hear the echoes of their cries and screams followed by a quick and subsequent crashing sound. Some residents have gone around to find the source, only to find the street chillingly empty and no cart or men anywhere. The event keeps on reliving itself.

The energy of the battle in some ways carries on at Fort Griswold each day, even centuries later. The stories of each heroic man and woman, the feelings and intense dedication to their nation, seeped into the ground, and to step into the park that is now Fort Griswold in Groton is to step foot into a battle that precipitated one of the founding acts of America. To walk the streets of New London is to walk where heroes, privateers and rebels abounded and fought for life when their former brother and ally came with mighty flame to take them down. It is believed that deaths of violence and intensity, as well as deaths in the face of deep belief and protection, can be the kinds that create the most real and tangible ghosts. Fort Griswold proves this to be true. New London proves this to be true. Although each man and woman left a legacy, none of this would have happened without Connecticut's own Benedict Arnold turning on his own men close to home. It is nearly impossible to imagine the destruction he saw at his own hands that day.

What a spectacularly horrendous image to behold indeed. Arnold was in the city for much of the burning, but local legend and historical documentation has it that he went up the hill on what is now called Hempstead Street to the town's Antientist Burial Ground and stood on the hillside near the grave of Admiral Shaw's father, peering through a spyglass at the events unfolding. From that cemetery hill, surrounded by those who had passed before him, settling the great city of New London, he could see the burning of the buildings at his feet—the city that had molded him as a boy, guided by people he once knew. Arnold also had a perfect view of the bloody brawl that was just about to take place across the Thames at Fort Griswold—his new Loyalist allies fighting against his former friends, allies and compatriots. He would never witness anything like this again in his life.

None of this history can assert with any certainty that Arnold was coldblooded regarding the men and women who were once his friends. The day did not go at all how he expected. When approaching New London, he wanted only to burn down the places of provisions and weaponry—war strongholds. He had no intent to have innocents perish and the homes of citizens burned down. The gunpowder explosion had seen to that. Arnold also sent messages that he wanted the Loyalists under his command to withdraw from the battle at Groton Heights. He claimed that he saw the defenses the fort was equipped with (which are evidenced by the fact that it's the most intact fort from that time in the world today) and knew that the taking of it would not be as easy as he initially thought. He did not expect nearly two hundred men to be there: "On my gaining a height of ground in the rear of New London from which I had good prospect of Fort Griswold, I found it much more formidable than I expected."

He sent this message to Colonel Eyre as he stood on the hillside, getting a full view of what the fort looked like, but the message arrived too late. The battle had begun. Who is to say that the mere sight of the stellar fortification wasn't Arnold's valid reason to withdraw, but it stands to reason that perhaps he saw the men, the Patriots he once fought with, the small number of them bravely assembled to protect his home territory, and felt a twinge of guilt.

Ye Antientist Burial Ground and Nathan Hale Schoolhouse in New London, circa late 1800s and early 1900s. *Courtesy of New London Landmarks.*

This wasn't what he had expected in his wildest imagination. New London city was in flames, and those who were not so long ago his allies and friends would likely perish during such an uneven fight.

We may never know the true content of Benedict Arnold's heart in his alleged attempt to withdraw the men from battle and not burn down any more homes. But to this day, if you stand on that hillside in Ye Towne's Antientist Burial Ground—where Arnold stood watching the flames roar, the smoke rise, the cannonballs soar, the bullets fly and the blood pour—the energy is tangible, raw and real. The fearful intensity will send a chill up your spine, and for a brief instant, the sounds of traffic and chatter will die away and you will hear the yelling of men and the running of citizens and might see the ships of those evacuees taking off down the river in great escape as horror unfolded around them. Arnold was, after all, a person with feelings and attachments, as are we all, and an event like this unfolding at his hands would have left him forever touched, haunting his mind as it continues to haunt the land.

September 6, 1781, is a date that will live in infamy in the Constitution State, a date when men fought one of the bloodiest battles ever to take place on Connecticut soil in an effort to secure freedom. It is a date when

View of Fort Griswold as Benedict Arnold would have seen it in 1781 from Ye Antientist Burial Ground in New London, circa 2015.

Ye Antientist Burial Ground in New London, circa 2015.

a traitor would surprise even himself with the havoc that his efforts would wreak on land he knew so well. Men and women would set themselves apart as unbelievable strongholds in the fight for what they believed in. The Revolutionary War would conclude less than a year later, making this one of the final battlegrounds and massacre sites of this pivotal time. The Battle at Yorktown, Virginia, would commence just weeks later amid the rebel cries to "Remember New London!" as they bombarded their enemy. The destruction wrought on the Connecticut city ignited such rage and motivated Patriots across the land to conquer the red coats in their next, largest battleground of the war. Fort Griswold has been and always will be a place that will forever harbor the history and the ghosts within it as a reminder to us all of those who forged the way for the life we have today.

Note: The monument at Fort Griswold as seen in photographs did not stand at the time of this battle. This was built in 1826 and dedicated in 1830 with a top enclosure added years later in 1881.

New London

The Unsung Stories of Heroes and Heroines

Shaw Mansion

When venturing up Blinman Street in New London, you may feel instantly transported back centuries in time as your eyes gaze at a mansion built of strong granite, mighty in structure and awe-inspiring in appearance. Atop a small hillside, the mansion's view overlooks the waterways of New London's Thames River. In the yard behind, a picturesque gazebo sits in a perfectly manicured garden. "Wow, what impressive people must live here," you must be thinking. But if you peer ever so closely to the sign that hangs just above the doorway, you will see the words proudly boasting who this beautiful structure belongs to: the New London County Historical Society. That is the organization now headquartered at this prestigious site. Currently, it is a museum filled with the artifacts of those who came before, but it is also so much more. It was a standout home for a well-to-do but brave, independence-driven family for hundreds of years before its incarnation as a historical society (as donated and wished for by the last remaining descendant, who had inherited the property and donated it as a museum in 1907).

So many names are thought of when thinking of Revolutionary War history. Names of great men and some stories are left seemingly untold, known only to locals and enthusiasts for the time. Some would say that such is the story of the fierce, indomitable and heroic Shaw family. Their role in the American Revolutionary War and beyond forever changed the events and outcomes of the late eighteenth century.

Shaw Mansion in New London, circa late 1890s and early 1900s. *Courtesy of New London County Historical Society, New London, Connecticut.*

This granite structure, known fondly as Shaw Mansion, is named, of course, after the family who built it and called it home for more than two hundred years. The structure was built in 1756 by Captain Nathaniel Shaw and an assembled group of refugees from Nova Scotia. Indeed, in the 1750s, there was an influx of refugees from the north, and when they arrived in Connecticut, they were limited in their occupational options. Captain Shaw, a man of means, provided employment to the refugees as he moved to transition what was once a small wooden structure for a home into the stone mansion it became. In 1756, the home had reached completion, and the small wooden structure that once served as a homestead of much less grandeur became an addition—repurposed in a sense. Some say that this was an office space at one time; however, this was later during the Revolution, when Captain Shaw's son had taken over the homestead. But at that time of the mansion's construction, the small wooden structure was documented to be a kitchen addition to the mansion.

Captain Nathaniel Shaw had always led a seafaring life, and that is indeed what brought him to New London. He spent many years a sea captain in the trade of Irish linens. It was indeed his frequent travels to Ireland that is thought to have inspired and influenced the structure and décor of his outstanding new home. In every single room, he utilized a plaster not seen in common furnishings or houses anywhere outside the Emerald Isle. Irish roots can still be felt today within the Shaw Mansion's plaster-lined surfaces. Captain Shaw had been married to his wife, Temperance Harris, for twenty-six years prior to the home's completion, and they both spent the remainder of their years together within the mansion's walls—twenty-two more years for the dear captain, who passed away in 1778, and forty for Temperance, who passed away in 1796. They had eight children together, six sons and two daughters; three of the sons perished at sea in varying years but all of young ages, in their early twenties. Sadly, this was a common story in New London, where so many families of a seafaring trade lost their loved ones to the ocean's mysterious depths. Both daughters died tragically young as well, only at ages twenty-five and twenty-four, respectfully. Sarah had been married to a man named David Allen at the time of her passing, and Mary, the youngest, was married to Reverend Ephraim Woodbridge at the time of her passing; she was the only one who left any descendants to the Shaw family. Three sons lived until middle age, including the distinguished and unforgettable Nathaniel Shaw Jr.

Nathaniel Shaw Jr. was, like his father, a man of the sea and also a man of independence. He spent his years supporting the same war efforts his father had in life. Lucky for Nathaniel Shaw Jr., his father had become one of the wealthiest merchants in New London, and he was to inherit an incredibly successful business in 1763 at the completion of the Seven Years' War, when trade resumed once more. Like his father, he was assisting in organizing New London's efforts in the war. As a man of means, he was able to garner much influence over his neighbors and friends, given their ability to sustain a rebel stronghold. He became a very important figure of the American Revolution, particularly in Connecticut.

Nathaniel Jr. and his wife, Lucretia, were also adamant supporters of the education of the young in their community and were trustees and benefactors of the nearby Union School of New London, now known as the Nathan Hale Schoolhouse of New London. Nathan Hale became schoolmaster there in 1774 and was there for about one year, into 1775. It was during this time that he became good friends with Nathaniel and Lucretia Shaw. They even appeared to be supporters of young Hale's unique initiative to teach young ladies as well as young men. Hale's relationship with the Shaws quickly blossomed, and he was a frequent guest at the Shaw Mansion for meals with the distinguished couple. Shaw was in full support later when Hale resigned his post at the school and went on to become a member and of the Seventh Connecticut Regiment as a lieutenant, gifting him powder and shot at his departure.

In 1776, the Continental Congress got together and made the decision that it needed a navy, but funding was an issue, so it floated an idea. It enlisted the assistance in each state for the formation of a navy, and every state had an appointed naval agent. Nathaniel Shaw Jr. became the appointed naval agent for the entire state of Connecticut. His commissioning letter can still be viewed at the mansion today. The home soon partially served as an official early American naval office. For this appointment, the Continental Congress at the time supplied him with four ships. The remainder of his merchant ships became ships used exclusively for privateering. As Kayla Correll, assistant director of the New London County Historical Society, so eloquently noted during a tour of the mansion, privateering in the 1700s should not be confused with pirate behavior of pillaging, storming and destroying. Privateers had a strict code of ethics that they were to abide by, and when they seized a ship, their purpose was to take contraband for the war effort where it was needed and send the rest to public auction. Nothing could be kept for personal gain. There was indeed a law for privateering. Shaw utilized these resources quite effectively to garner as many supplies as possible and evade British blockades. Eric Lehman documented, "He acquired flour and coffee, shoes and uniforms, gunpowder and shot. He dealt with the loss of his own ships and the acquisition of prize ships. He tried to respond to urgent requests from Washington for supplies or information." Shaw Mansion even houses a letter in its collection today that is proudly displayed, addressed to Nathaniel Shaw Jr. from General George Washington himself, expressing deep gratitude for the contraband provided.

Near the time of Nathaniel Jr.'s appointment as naval agent, he, wife Lucretia, the whole hospitable family and the staff of the Shaw Mansion played host to General Washington himself. Washington was moving his troops from Cambridge, and on his way through, he found rest at the Shaw Mansion, dining with the family and putting his head down for the night. The room in which he stayed was the master bedroom, belonging then to Captain Shaw and Temperance. Today, that room is fondly named the Washington Room after the general, in honor of his stay that April evening. Indeed, the spirit of Washington is often felt or remarked about concerning the items that he was close to during his stay. The large three-section banquet table where he ate his dinner with the Shaws sits proudly in the dining room. Perhaps most unique of all is the mirror that hangs in the Washington Room. It is the mirror the good general would have shaved in and looked into during his stay. That mirror has never been moved out of the house and is where Washington would have used it. Local historian, author and consultant Jennifer Emerson points this out when tours of schoolchildren happily proceed through the mansion. They can't help but be captivated by the mirror, and when they find out that their first president looked into that mirror, Ms. Emerson can observe them looking into it as if they may find him there.

It is indeed common spiritual belief that if you look into a mirror at night holding only a candlelight, you can see the spirit of someone who has passed. This inspires the thought that just maybe a little piece of each person who looks into a mirror is left behind. Perhaps that is what the candlelight gives you a glimpse of.

As the schoolchildren gaze into the mirror, looking for the general himself, some of them will even address him personally as if he is right in the room. "Good morning, General Washington!" they will proudly exclaim and then run back to Jennifer to say, "I saw him. I saw him! He's in there." Excited children letting their imagination and hopes get the best of them? Quite possibly. But just perhaps, with their open minds and willingness to embrace those who have walked before, General Washington does pop through that window into the home in which he stayed that spring of 1776, just to say hello to the children who adore him. When the children inquire of Ms. Jennifer if she believes him present, she always has the same response: "I hope this home provided him with a much-needed rest, and I hope of all the places he stayed in his life that he remembers fondly that his night in the mansion was one of them." This response puts a smile on their faces and leaves it up to each and every one of us, children or grown, to decide if General Washington still visits his friends at the Shaw Mansion.

Traveling back to the late eighteenth century after General Washington's visit and the appointment of Shaw as a naval agent of the Nutmeg State, work was going well for the Shaws. Large amounts of contraband were sent from New London to the war efforts up and down the coast. It seems that the good general couldn't have picked a better choice than Nathaniel Shaw Jr. In July 1780, when five thousand French troops under Rochambeau landed in Newport, Rhode Island (a Loyalist stronghold and still under British control), they required immense amounts of supplies. Shaw did as he always had, responding to the general's requests as swiftly and efficiently as possible. It was during this time, however, that tensions ran remarkably high and Washington seemed a bit unnerved. He requested that Shaw serve not as a spy but rather as an intelligence gatherer, watching the movements of the British on the Long Island Sound. He trusted no one more than Shaw. Washington left infantry men in a close radius around Shaw in order to gain information as quickly as possible.

This was successful for a time, with Shaw even able to get intelligence delivered to the French in Newport. Weeks later, the infamous Benedict Arnold would be found out as a traitor, but until then, in late July/early August, he was an assumed ally who also reached out to Shaw looking for assistance and expressing an interest in privateering. Shaw obliged and did his best to see what he could do to help out Mr. Arnold, but the cost that he would need to incur to do was, according to Arnold, too great an expense. It was the last documented interaction between Arnold and Shaw, at least on friendly terms. Suffice it to say, Arnold knew all about Shaw, his business, the privateering and varying ins and outs of the Shaw family trade when he planned his raid on New London a year later. The Shaw Mansion's place as a naval office on the direct route from each major city in the Northeast to the next made the mansion a hot spot for all such matters of the era.

The Shaw family seemingly knew all the key players (General Washington, Nathan Hale, Benedict Arnold, Governor Trumbull, Governor Griswold,

Shaw Mansion in New London, circa 1930s. *Courtesy of New London County Historical Society, New London, Connecticut.*

General Greene and Marquis de Lafayette) of Revolutionary America. The family were just as key as all the guests and friends they hosted at their mansion, corresponded with or encountered in their work. The Shaws were trusted, and trust is not easy to come by. The Shaw family efforts were decidedly crucial to the success of the rebels in the American Revolution.

The Battle at Groton Heights and the Burning of New London on September 6, 1781, became the ultimate test of Lucretia's fortitude, to say the least. Lucretia was always in full support of her husband, assisting in any way that she could. Primarily, Lucretia served a nurse to the wounded and abused prisoners who were released or even escaped from British jails throughout the area. Covered in human waste, blood, sweat and tears and beaten sometimes beyond recognition, they made their way for assistance back to their homes throughout New London city and the surrounding area. Lucretia went to care for them no matter how ghastly their appearance or fateful their diagnosis, lending a helping hand and tending their needs and, if possible, nursing them back to health.

Sometimes, Lucretia would even utilize part of the Shaw Mansion as a makeshift hospital for the sick and wounded Patriots of the war. In particular, this is exactly what happened after the Battle at Groton Heights. During the Burning of New London and the Battle at Groton Heights, Lucretia's husband was off innocently on a hunting expedition, having no idea what horrors lie ahead. By the time of his departure and the witnessing of Arnold and 1,600 British arriving, it was too late—he had been blockaded from returning and felt helpless. Lucretia was at home with their staff and some other family members. Shaw Mansion was the first stop on newly turned Arnold's list. The *Hannah*, the ship that had been seized by Shaw's privateers, was at the end of his dock, and it was the reason why Arnold and the men were ordered to go to New London. They were to go and retrieve it. Whether it was rage or a thought-out plan all his own, Arnold arrived and set fire to the *Hannah*, docked on Shaw's property right there in the harbor. The mansion was then the first building he set fire to as he proceeded into town with the men—a pointed, personal attack, it seemed.

Lucretia had seen them coming and knew that her husband was unable to be there. She quickly ran into his office (the small wooden structure that had once been the kitchen) and gathered as many important books and papers as she could manage before the flames overtook the place. The servants were of great assistance. Unfortunately, the chest containing many of the naval office's official papers perished, but she had done great work nonetheless. But what about the house? Would she have to flee? A neighbor whose house was spared and passed by the British came to the Shaw Mansion's rescue and helped to extinguish the fire immediately. Thus, the only casualty of any kind at Shaw Mansion on that fateful day was the original wooden structure that had once been the family homestead and had become an addition. The beautiful stone mansion overlooking the harbor remained intact.

The greatest casualties and effects of this day were yet to come. Lucretia did not let panic set in. She knew the Shaw family's reputation, and without her husband home, she, as the lady of the house, would have had to do everything possible to show their support to the men, the volunteers and the rebels who were out there defending their hometown, fighting still for their independence—a cause to which she was completely devoted. The homestead would become a hospital, and although many injured made it to the Avery House, others still made it to the Shaw Mansion, where she and staff cared for them and tended to their wounds, thanking them for all of their efforts. After the British had left, her husband, Nathan, was able to return home. He was one of the many men who went to the fort to retrieve survivors and help pick up the proverbial and literal pieces.

Lucretia's act of care and devotion for all those men committed to the cause was the beginning of her final grand act. A true lady she was until the end. In providing care for these men, she contracted a fever. Author and Daughter of the American Revolution member Jennifer Emerson stated that it seemed she most likely contracted viral meningitis—at the time, they may have simply called it a "brain fever." The lady of the house, Mrs. Lucretia Harris Shaw, passed away on December 11, 1781, just two weeks before Christmas. She passed having seemingly reaped the repercussions of surrounding herself with wounded, sickly men. An intelligent woman, we must admit that she likely knew the risks and knew them to be worthwhile. That's how much the cause meant to her. She gave her life to the cause, but not until after she had fearlessly and devoutly cared for those who risked their lives for the independence in which they all believed. A fire screen that she was embroidering at the time of her death remained unfinished and was put on display by her family members. It is a family heirloom deeply valued by Jane and is seen as the last relic of a true martyr. It remains in the museum today.

Nathaniel Jr. was, of course, devastated and heartbroken by the loss of his dear wife, but he was a pillar of strength in his community. He was still needed in the remaining months of the war, and given that it was such a dire and pivotal time for the fledgling nation, he did his best to carry on. Tragically, only four months later, during a duck hunting trip with some friends, Nathaniel lost his life. The events that transpired that day are shrouded in mystery. When the fatal shot was fired, Nathaniel was alone; the shot went into his ribs. He was brought home to the Shaw Mansion by his request to die at home and finalize his will. He survived three days after the accidental shooting before he passed away on April 12, 1782. To this day, we may never know for sure if grief took over the man of immense fortitude and the wound was self-inflicted or if indeed it was some strange accident. A man of fierce and admirable willpower held out long enough to make sure all his affairs were in order. His slaves were freed and his will completed. He passed away in his own home, in his own bed, as had his wife before him. Their bedroom had become the master bedroom by this time, the room known today as the Washington Room. Perhaps their joint energies also account for some of the intensity that can be felt when entering that very chamber. They were a couple of amazing fortitude during the rise of a new nation, and they were a support system that the community would sorely miss. Mrs. Emerson remarked that all of this is exactly what they should be remembered for, stating, "They had a commitment to what they believed in and were true Patriots. They had a commitment to one another and the cause of independence. Lucretia Shaw should be remembered as a martyr to her country."

Nathaniel Jr. and Lucretia Shaw were buried among family, side by side under distinguished tabletop gravestones (indicating just how important and wealthy they were, to say the least) at Ye Towne's Antientist Burial Ground on Hempstead Street. Their site overlooks the Thames River, and you can't hold but a certain amount of awe and reverence when visiting. The local Daughters of the American Revolution, Lucretia Shaw Chapter, pays tribute to its namesake, Lucretia, every year with a wreath-laying ceremony. When you go to visit Mrs. Lucretia Shaw, as evidenced in EVP audio recording sessions, you can hear the lilt of her beautiful songlike voice whispering through a wind, even on windless days. When a visitor arrives to the cemetery, so do Lucretia and Nathaniel, as if to say, "Thank you for remembering me."

The house remained in the family from 1756 to 1907, passing ultimately to the children of Nathaniel Jr.'s sister, Mary, and then her children and their children afterward. During this time, prestigious visitors continued to arrive, including the Marquis de Lafayette, who came in 1824 to visit the remaining members of the Shaw family. As they reminisced of Nathaniel Jr. and Lucretia and their valiant efforts back in the century past, Lafayette told them something remarkable. The Battle at Yorktown was only a mere matter

Entrance sign of Ye Antientist Burial Ground in New London, circa 2015.

of weeks after the massacre at Groton Heights, and while leading troops in battle there, he called out to them, "Remember New London." Many of them repeated this in chorus as they charged the enemy. The sentiment and the motivation were pure and would certainly do the memory of the Shaw family proud. Most certainly, they were smiling down on their home when Lafayette delivered this proud news.

Jennifer Emerson, a true Renaissance woman of many talents, is also an actress and frequently portrays Lucretia and Nathaniel's great-grandniece, Jane Perkins, who left the home to the New London County Historical Society in 1907, years before her passing in 1930. She was the last of the ancestral line to inherit and reside in the Shaw Mansion. As a welcoming gift to the historical society in 1907, the family presented it with an unexpected find: an original thirteen-star flag, of which only ten remain in the world. The Smithsonian doesn't have one. After Jane Perkins left the historical society, members were looking in the attic when they saw something wedged in between two glass pieces. It was revealed to be the thirteen-star flag, hand-sewn silk, probably never flown but displayed prominently in Nathaniel Jr.'s office. The flag is also not the traditional Betsy Ross flag, with stars in a circle. It seemed to mimic in a way the Shaw family crest of a circle with three symbols in the middle and ten stars forming a circle around three in the center. The original artifact is on display at the house in New London to this day alongside numerous other relics—some mentioned before and some pieces that were taken from privateering expeditions and never left family hands.

The mansion and its gracious family hosted many people of prominence during the Revolutionary era and even through its later years when it saw Greek Revival renovations and changes in its décor. The colonial air and energy of true nostalgia never left the mansion's secure walls. It seems that some of the residents didn't leave either, as their spirits are still often felt by visitors, volunteers and employees alike. There seems to be a broad consensus about a few things regarding spirit activity at the mansion: it is always with good will, no malice; it is always an intense energy of seeming approval; it is friendly; and most of the time it is distinctly female (perhaps the lady of the house herself, Mrs. Lucretia Shaw). Volunteer Marilyn Davis remarked, "We always call the spirit Lucretia. Even if nothing happens—which often it doesn't—whenever we lock up for the day and head toward the door, we commonly say goodbye to Lucretia and let her know we'll see her soon." She continued, "When entering the house alone, we usually just let Lucretia

Shaw Mansion street view in New London. *Photo by Shelby McInvale.*

know that it's us and what we're coming to do." While they may not hear or see it, there is the distinct sense that Lucretia hears them when they speak to her in the home and, in a way, responds.

Sometimes it seems that Lucretia is still trying to assist in the management of her home, still acting as head of household, knowing what events are going on and what needs to be done. A previous librarian at the Shaw Mansion, Tricia Royston, had a very interesting encounter. Her story, as told by Assistant Director Kayla Correll, is that Tricia would remark that sometimes items would seem to go missing. You could spend hours or days looking for an item in the mansion's large square footage and come up empty-handed. But Lucretia, it seemed, would be watching and obliged to help. One day, Tricia saw a stapler on an exhibit case, loosely placed and purposeless. She had not put it there, and neither had anyone else in the homestead. The stapler's home is always the podium found near the front door of the mansion. Upon finding the out-of-place stapler, Tricia brought it back to the podium drawer to which it belonged. *Voila!* The item she had spent days searching for was right in the drawer in the spot where the stapler should have been. It wasn't left out openly, but she was directed right to where her lost item was. According to Tricia, occurrences like this are not infrequent at the Shaw Mansion.

The aforementioned Jennifer, who has spent much time at the mansion, has also had a few spiritual and mysterious events unfold during her work at the home. One day, Jennifer and her friends were strolling through the house and entered into the back hallway. They went to walk past the area through the Victorian-adorned bedroom where there is the door that leads to the attic space. As they were walking across the threshold into the bedroom, Jennifer's friend Penny was just passing the closed latch door when she heard a sound. She looked over at the door to see the old latch lift and the door slowly swing open, presenting her the stairs as if to say, "Come on up." It was an inviting sense. Was it Lucretia or Jane, perhaps? Whoever was up there gave them a bit of a startle, but there was still a calm and assured air that gave them the sense that all was well.

Ms. Emerson also noted that during any Revolutionary War–era event that the museum, society or city puts on, the house seems to come alive and the energy of mansion kicks into overdrive. At every New London Food Stroll, the Ancient Mariner's War of 1812 Fife and Drum Corps parades up and down the street playing patriotic tunes, and without fail, it always arrives at the door of the Shaw Mansion to play a patriotic set of tunes. As the fife and drum corps play, the intensity of the energy becomes palpable. Jennifer, standing there clad as Jane Perkins, feels the spiritual energy surround her in a swarm as the spirits affirm that they are thrilled to be remembered. They know that tribute is being paid to them. How extraordinary. At a recent food stroll, as Jennifer stood on the front porch in full costume, she could feel someone standing close to her. It was the distinct feeling that she was standing on the spot where Lucretia would've stood as mistress of the house to welcome any honored guest, including General Washington.

Similarly, after another annual food stroll and evening of paying honor to the Shaws had passed, it was time to close up the mansion for the evening. As Jennifer and her colleague did so and made their way down the stairs to their vehicles, having made sure that everything was shut off and locked up tight, they noticed something outside of their peripheral vision. A light in the attic was on, brightly emanating from the mansion. Jennifer was a little bit wary; she loved the home, but at night, the feeling that it didn't belong to the living any longer was always so clear. She didn't want to have to go back in there alone to shut off that light. She gave her colleague a worried look, and she backed up the sentiment, saying that she would not go back in there either. After a brief discussion, Jennifer convinced her colleague that they would go back in together, turn off the attic light and leave. Jennifer walked into the mansion and addressed the spirits of the Shaw family: "This is what's happening, everyone. I am coming in to shut the attic light off, and then we are leaving. Don't worry. It's fine. We are not staying. You will have your house back, and we apologize for the inconvenience."

Jennifer flew up the stairs as fast as her feet could carry her, hit that light switch and swiftly exited the Shaw Mansion for the evening. The funny thing is that they both remember the light being off before they walked back to the door. Had the spirits turned it back on? If so, which one? It is hard to say, but their presence was distinct.

That's something Jennifer is accustomed to. After leading a school group through, she will close up the shutters and walk out of the room, but on her final glance, she will sometimes notice that a shutter remains open. Certain that she had closed it, she goes back to the shutter, closes it once more and walks out. It seems again perhaps just a friendly greeting. During reenactments as Ms. Perkins, you may notice that Jennifer Emerson no longer exists; it will feel distinctly as if Ms. Perkins in in the room with you. That's what a true actress does, right? Surely, but sometimes it seems that Jane and Lucretia are standing right nearby and will even dispense words of wisdom if need be. One time, an audience member inquired of Miss Perkins (Jennifer) what she thought of Benedict Arnold. Jennifer felt a rush

Shaw Mansion garden view in New London. *Photo by Shelby McInvale.*

of electricity charge her entire body as she heard a voice exit her mouth that said, "I prefer not to discuss it." It wasn't until after she heard those words exit her lips that she realized they weren't her own. In an effort to educate the public, she would've normally given a more verbose response, but Lucretia, the lady of the house who knew the man and knew the repercussions of his acts firsthand, gave the most ladylike response of all.

At the Shaw Mansion, you may find yourself so taken with the artifacts and ambience that you cannot break yourself away from the energy present. Indeed, you may find yourself glancing into the mirror that George Washington, Lucretia Shaw or Nathaniel Shaw Jr. once gazed into and see their reflections. You may stroll past the fire screen that Lucretia never finished, hear footsteps around you that you can't place, see a door creak open on its own and maybe even feel someone standing near you, brimming with gratitude that you came to learn of them. Know that their spirits are gracious and welcoming. If on the off chance you see a light on in the dead of night as you walk up Blinman Street, you may think, "Hey, someone made a mistake." But think twice—perhaps they didn't, and the house has come alive with the spirits of the Shaw family and Revolutionary America in downtown New London.

Hempsted Houses

Just a quarter of a mile westward in New London on the namesake Hempstead Street, you will find another unique museum that has stood the test of time since 1678, nearly one hundred years before the beginning of the Revolutionary War. Two unique houses sit on the property once belonging to the Hempstead family, with additions and a second home being added throughout the year. The original home appears like no other. The house is a frame structure reminiscent of English medieval style. There is a pitched side-gable roof, an expansive central chimney and diamond-pane windows. If you think that part of the house may appear a bit differently than this, you would be right. There was an addition in 1728 to the 1678 house that was more modern in style, with sash windows and a variant shingle.

The earliest and most notable documentation of life in the house and within the Hempstead family came from Joshua Hempstead's diary. Joshua Hempstead Jr., whose parents, Joshua and Elizabeth, had the house built in 1678, was born that same year, on September 1. He would live his entire life in that home, and the second house on the very property made purely of

The 1678 Joshua Hempsted House in New London, circa 1940. *Courtesy of the Library of Congress.*

picturesque stone was built by his son Nathaniel in 1728. Joshua Hempstead, fondly called "the diarist" by many for his detailed accounts of colonial life in New London, was married to Abigail Bailey of Long Island when he was just twenty years old, in 1698. The next year, their family began to grow, and together they had nine children. Tragically, only a few days after giving birth to their ninth child, and only five days after their eldest son, Joshua (the third), had passed away, Abigail subsequently passed away as well.

A widower, Joshua Hempstead Jr. never remarried and instead devoted his life to bringing up his children and continuing to work for their well-being. He served in various trades over the years, allowing him to maintain the grand home. He worked as a shipwright, carpenter, lawyer, surveyor and business agent. First and foremost, however, his trade was that of a farmer. Joshua Jr.'s legacy is detailed in his written work, and he discusses all matters, including life in the merchant business in New London and Protestant revivalism. That Protestant belief was strong in the family throughout the generations. His diary was kept from 1711 to 1758, just six weeks before he passed away. A man of great knowledge, connections and travel, his legacy carries on in New London today, and the Hempstead name grew only more recognizable as the events of the later eighteenth century and the Revolutionary War began to unfold.

Two Hempstead descendants would go on to be part of the Revolutionary War—one in a large and unprecedented way. Diarist Joshua Jr.'s grandson, Stephen Hempstead, born on May 6, 1754, to his father (also named Stephen Hempstead) and mother (Sarah Holt), became a local icon. He was known as a hero for his fierce bravery, shown at Fort Griswold in the Battle of Groton Heights, and also for his time spent serving as a sergeant in the Seventh Connecticut Regiment under Connecticut state hero and martyr Lieutenant Nathan Hale (later promoted to the rank of captain), who had recruited him during his time living in New London. This took place shortly after Hale's resignation as schoolmaster of Union School and not long after General Washington's visit. A letter from school friend Benjamin Tallmadge arrived fervently encouraging Hale to join the cause with full heart.

Hempstead had grown up in the Hempsted House (the structure spelled without the *a* in honor of later generations) as it is seen today, and it was always considered his "home." That is where he was living when he and Hale first became acquainted with each other and when he was ultimately recruited. Hempstead had always looked up to Hale and idolized him in a way. Only a year younger than Nathan—Stephen just nineteen years old and Nathan only twenty—they became fast and trusted comrades. Hale and

Hempstead served together for about a year in the Seventh Connecticut Regiment, spending time also in divided places across what is now the New York City area. By 1776, Hale was feeling more ambitious, desiring to be something more than the captain he had become. Despite hesitancy and misgivings by his friends, Hale made his decision. He would respond to Washington's request for intelligence gatherers and become a spy.

Sergeant Stephen Hempstead stood strongly by his side, and when Hale made his decision, they departed Harlem Heights together and made their way to Norwalk, Connecticut. Hale told Captain Pond of Norwalk about his orders, and then the two gentlemen made their way back across the sound to Long Island. Upon arrival in Huntington, the double agent was revealed. Hale removed his colonial uniform, dressed in a plain suit and pretended to be a schoolmaster. The only personal belonging he took with him was his Yale diploma, to aid him in maintaining this ruse. It was time for Stephen Hempstead and Nathan Hale to part ways for the final time.

Stephen was not to be a spy. Instead, he went on to leave his own legacy in other ways. However, Sergeant Hempstead was requested by Nathan to return some items to the family should he not survive, including a trunk of his personal belongings, private papers and, perhaps most notably, his silver shoe buckles. He could not wear those when walking around as poor Dutch schoolmaster—the shoe buckles would be a dead giveaway that he was a spy, or at least not a teacher. Hempstead returned to Norwalk, and later he ventured back to eastern Connecticut and subsequently Coventry, where he proudly took the honor of carrying Nathan's belongings back to his family's homestead in Coventry after Nathan was captured and hanged for treason as a spy on September 22, 1776. Admittedly, it is believed that Hempstead held on to the shoe buckles for a bit after the news, having difficulty parting with his dear friend. They were always a reminder to Hempstead of his good friend and personal hero. To this day, the shoe buckles sit on display at the Hale Homestead in Coventry, Connecticut, although some argue that the Hempsted Houses wouldn't be a bad place to display them either, in honor of the friendship Stephen and Nathan once had.

By the next year, as the Revolutionary War was in full swing, Stephen Hempstead continued to serve as part as the Seventh Connecticut Regiment and still served time in New York, where so much activity took place. By the age of twenty-three, he continued his service to the Patriots in their pursuit for independence and was a fierce participant in the Battle of Harlem Heights. During an attack of an enemy ship, Hempstead was shot with grapeshot, shattering two of his ribs. After this injury, he was stationed

Portrait of Stephen Hempstead, circa late 1700s and early 1800s. *Courtesy of the* St. Louis Post-Dispatch.

in familiar territory—he had finally made his way back to his home of New London and continued to assist under Colonel Ledyard at Forts Trumbull and Griswold. The Ledyards and Hempsteads had a close relationship, and Sergeant Hempstead and Colonel Ledyard took charge of the southeastern Connecticut strongholds and fortifications, fighting for and defending their independence. For a few years, this worked well. By the time Stephen was twenty-seven years old, he was still serving in the regiment, married, had children and was living with his family not far from the family homestead—the Hempsted Houses in which he had grown up. This was the year, 1781, of the fateful Burning of New London and the Battle at Groton Heights at the hands Benedict Arnold and his 1,600 "loyal American soldiers."

As dawn broke, Hempstead spotted the ships in the harbor at New London and promptly reported to his post at Fort Trumbull, ready and willing to defend it to the death if need be. Most of the men were at Fort Griswold, where most of the battle took place, but an effort had to be made at Fort Trumbull, even if was a slight deterrence. Hempstead and twenty-two other men killed a handful of British soldiers with grapeshot from Fort Trumbull as they approached on foot from the street. They spiked their cannons and piled into boats, making their way bravely to Fort Griswold—or at least they attempted to do so. The British were able to capture one of the boats as it was taking off and stopped those rebels from making it across. However, Stephen made it safely to the site of what was to be a battle of epic proportions never before seen in Connecticut. Everyone assembled at Fort Griswold was thrilled for Stephen's arrival. He was experienced and an expert when it came to cannon firing.

Stephen Hempstead took his station at the gate to take charge of firing the cannons, but he was immediately struck by a musket ball, which grazed his head just above his ear and caused him to lose a profuse amount of blood. He and his fellow men bound the wound with a handkerchief, and

Hempstead bravely charged on, refusing to let this stop him from defending his city and his people's independence. Moments after Hempstead charged forward and grabbed a pike, he was struck again. The British must surely have been astonished by his resilience, but this time they got him in the arm. However, Stephen Hempstead, as bloodied and injured as he was, picked himself back up, retrieved the spear he had dropped upon being shot and charged forward to clear the breach. His comrades proudly stood beside him and assisted his astonishing actions. The battle, however, had just begun, and Hempstead knew that this was the beginning for all of them. The defenders were winning, but this was short-lived. The Patriots were outnumbered at least six to one, and they couldn't keep the odds in their favor forever. Colonel Ledyard moved to surrender. As if to mock him for deciding this too late, the British took Ledyard's surrendered sword and stabbed him with it, killing him in front of all his men. This sent Stephen Hempstead into a rage. He and the others stormed the British with all their might. As he did so, he was stabbed in the right hip just above the joint; for the time being, at least, he was unable to walk but still alive.

Hempstead's torturous day of watching his comrades die and physically tortured and almost killed was not over. As he lay there, his blood running out over the earth, the battle ended to the defenders' defeat, and the British began to gather the injured into a cart or a wheelbarrow of sorts so that they could become prisoners. The British soldier in charge of pushing the ammunition cart lost control, and the casualties were thrust down a steep embankment and crashed into a tree. The cart burst and the men fell, Stephen included. After Colonel Ledyard's kin, Ebenezer Ledyard, convinced the British to parole at least some of the injured, including Hempstead, it seemed that he might have a chance to survive. Hempstead and other survivors were brought to the Avery House, where he was found by the innocent Fanny Ledyard. He was bloodied beyond recognition and lay there dying, with wounds all over his body. Ledyard prepared him hot chocolate, warmed his body and his soul and tended to his wounds. He was nursed back to health by varying doctors and did not die that day. In fact, Hempstead wouldn't die for fifty more years, at the ripe old age of seventy-seven.

It took Stephen eleven months to recover, and he lived out the rest of his life with a limp due to the grave injury above his hip. Stephen moved back to the family homestead, known today as the Hempsted House, because his physical body was not the only thing that sustained injuries that day. His separate family home where he had been living with his wife and children was burned to the ground in the Burning of New London. He stayed a few more years at the homestead in New London and continued his farmwork. He maintained his farming trade into his elderly age, after which he moved out to Missouri, where he lived the final years of his life. Likely he left, as many did, because New London entered an economic depression after the burning, and its revival would not come until the whaling industry began to take off and thrive in the 1820s. Stephen Hempstead received a pension until his later years for injuries sustained during the battle. Documentation of the horror-filled events can be found in his two personal accounts of it—one written shortly after the battle and another a document recounting the events in order to receive the pension from the government.

Stephen wasn't the only Hempstead who left a legacy as a Patriot of the family in the American Revolution. His elder cousin John Hempstead, son of his uncle John, also lived at the Hempsted House and was there for a time when these events unfolded. On September 6, 1781, John Hempstead, then about forty years old, was perhaps the first to observe Benedict Arnold and his men's arrival on New London's shores. John had joined the company of a few dozen armed New London men after his valiant effort to summon Colonel Harris. The armed men he accompanied had stationed themselves by the water, where they could clearly see the redcoats descend on their city. John presumably saw Benedict Arnold himself at the forefront of one of the ships. As the 1,600 Brits began to disembark their vessels near Fort Trumbull, John Hempstead and others fell back out of the forefront. They were in no position to take these men as the small ensemble they were at the time.

John was caught in the crossfire for a time as he made his way back home. When he arrived home, he encountered his cousin and local captain and hero Saltonstall calmly imbibing their gin, as if perhaps it would be their last glass. The only thing worse than death would be if the British were able to retrieve their liquor, so they hid it in a potato field among the weeds and proceeded to defend their city—priorities, of course. In addition to this, other Hempstead men were hiding rum in the basement in the hopes of hiding it from the British as well. At the end of the day, the Hempsted House remained intact, and all the liquor was stealthily and successfully retrieved. The British, it seemed, never got their hands on the gin or the rum. They did help themselves to a meal, however. As the women and children fled the homestead to safety miles away in the woods, they had to leave behind a freshly prepared meal. Upon the British arrival to their home, although most things were left untouched, the freshly prepared meal was wiped clean from the plates. Some British soldiers certainly didn't leave their raid hungry. Mrs. Hempstead, who prepared the meal, speculated that it might have been her good cooking that saved the notable structure.

John's journey that day had just begun. He hid near the gin's secret space in a nearby field of corn, which disguised him more efficiently. From his hiding spot, he was able to fire at a number of British soldiers who walked by. He was quickly outnumbered, and they soon figured out where the shots were coming from. They pursued John, but he ran like the wind, past the potato field with the gin and out of sight, escaping every shot they loosed in his direction. He went back to the family homestead, hid ammunition, prepared weaponry, retrieved his father's important papers and belongings that he had inherited for safekeeping and fled once more. He was on the run but also prepared to attack whoever might halt his efforts. While hiding his father's papers in a nearby wooded area, he noticed the flames taking over the Shaw Mansion, but to his relief, he saw the neighbor come to the home's aid.

John Hempstead took down whatever soldiers he encountered, protecting Hempstead family relics all the while, and at the end of the raid and after

The 1678 Joshua Hempsted House in New London, circa 2016. *Photo by Shelby McInvale.*

the departure of the British, he made his way back to the family homestead. It was intact; his home and family were safe, it seemed. The house indeed seemed a beacon, a safe haven. One hundred people gathered there as a retreat away from the chaos and debris that had devastated so much of New London. He allowed them to seek refuge there, but his work wasn't done. After the British ships were safely out of sight, he got into his own boat and rowed across the Thames back and forth, merely observing the devastation around him. His cousin William Hempstead finally summoned him back home, where they ventured to the fields where John had killed and shot down redcoats. Their bodies lay there lifeless, proof that he had at least prevented some of them from causing havoc and provided a defense of his hometown. After seeing their cousins, John and William Hempstead shared in the salvaged gin together and celebrated that at least they still had their lives and had taken down some of the vicious invaders in their wake.

Without the brave role of Joshua Hempstead Jr.'s grandchildren, Stephen and John, the effects of September 6, 1781, on New London and Groton would've been quite different and likely worse for the Patriot side. Without Stephen Hempstead's war efforts for much of his early adulthood, his time with Hale and beyond, the colonials who sought so hard for independence would not have been able to witness the impeccable bravery and commitment that Stephen displayed. He was a role model for those who knew him, both young and old. He was a man of immense fortitude, bravery and resilience.

With every vivid and graphic history comes a certain amount of spiritual energies, both residual and active, that become embedded within the environment around them. For every unique, strong character that lives or even visits a home, an imprint is left—a little bit of their spirit for all of eternity. You can bet with certainty that the impact of the events that surrounded the Hempstead Homestead and the families who inhabited it left a haunting mark on the property; it is detectable within the very atmosphere of the home and museum site today. Staff members and guides of Connecticut Landmarks, which acquired the property in 1942 and can be thanked for its accurate restoration, sometimes report that a strange feeling takes over the house as night falls and the moon rises in the sky. It's a place with a strange vibe, a place where you just don't want to be alone.

I had the pleasure of conducting a joint paranormal investigation with associates from DKS Paranormal, Ghosts of New England Research Society (GONERS) and TAPS Home Team. It was a terribly humid July evening at a non-air-conditioned historic site, but every moment was breathtaking as historic artifacts surrounded us belonging to Hempsteads and local New

London–area residents of centuries past. Upon entering a room on the first floor—set up now as a sort of living quarters but quite likely a bedroom of sorts at one time or another in the eighteenth and/or nineteenth centuries for the generations of families that called the place home—there was a feeling of a distinct presence.

Little did the assembled group know that a full-bodied apparition would make itself known. Four of us, all ladies, assembled in the room, with a table at the center, a fireplace on the wall, a door to the basement, a portrait of Stephen near us and various items filling the room. As I sat in an old chair, I looked toward investigator Stacey Phillips of DKS Paranormal, whose back was near to the basement door—the basement that had once housed the hidden rum. It was apparent that she wasn't standing there alone. The lights were shut off, and everyone was asking questions of any Hempsteads or others that may be present in spirit form. A heaviness filled the room. Someone was there, and their presence commanded our attention. Stacey edged forward and to the side away from the presence that she felt but couldn't place. She could feel the masculine energy that was curious as to our purpose but needed to assert his stance and his power. As Stacey moved, I saw immediately why, as a full-bodied apparition emerged standing next to her. A man, tall and limber in a military uniform, was present in the room previously filled with just ladies. His face was older and worn; the years of life on him and the wrinkles on his face told the story of a man who had seen and conquered so much.

Slowly the man in his spirit form moved past Stacey into the center of the room. Stacey indicated as he moved past her that she could feel his authoritarian presence—it was not malicious but still intimidating. As the apparition entered into the center of the room, he seemed so real. Slowly but surely, he approached each investigator and looked her directly in the eyes, curious and hesitant. What was our purpose? Why hadn't we announced ourselves? Who were we all as women to address him in a matter of authority? He was in charge. As he approached each one of us, there was a distinct chill on the humid, sweaty evening, letting us know just how close he was. Too frightened and awestruck to move, we all let the man make his rounds and knew that he was just letting us know that this was his home and he was the one who would address us if he so chose. We stayed for a bit longer, all of us gathering slowly on one side of the room rather than the circle in which we began, so that the man could have his space.

After a time, his energy dissipated somewhat, and we ventured forward to other parts of the house, allowing him his space and thanking him for his

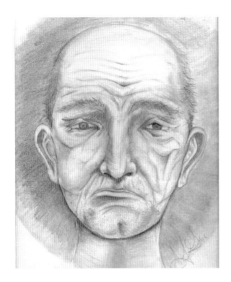

Portrait of the spirit at Hempsted Houses believed to be Stephen Hempstead. Sketch drawn by and provided courtesy of Madison E. Gish.

time. His presence was distinct, his power breathtaking and his authority unquestionable. With so many masculine presences having served as patriarch and head of household over the centuries, it is impossible to say with certainty exactly who this gentleman was, but his military appearance and intense strength of character do lend themselves to the type of man Stephen Hempstead would've been. And perhaps, since his portrait hung in that room alone, he sensed our enthusiasm to learn of his era and appeared for us. As the investigation continued, other strange things occurred. The dehumidifier on the stairwell to the second floor powered itself off for no reason. The feelings of mothers and children filled the second-floor bedroom, almost as if you could see the families living together and the care the mothers gave to their young. On the top floor, there was the sense of peace, having been a resting peace for servants and others.

The evening ended with time spent in the 1728 stone house, where energy of a spiritual kind emanated throughout the building. Small fluctuations in electromagnetic fields were indicated by the detectors that all the investigators carried, and as we stood on the second floor by a spinning wheel, imagining the work that was done in that room, a shadow was seen in the door. Again it was a male figure, this time holding a scythe, which was a bit scary at first glance. But the Hempsteads were a family with many farmers, so it stands to reason that we were encountering one of them just checking on the property.

The spirits of the Hempsted Houses had an undeniable presence, a reality to them that for a brief moment transported us back in time, through the veil. The history of the homes begins your journey, and the spirits complete it. If you visit the Hempstead family homestead, be sure to pay your respects and thank those who came before you and paved the way for independence in the American nation we know and love today.

New London is a city rich in antiquity and abundant in supernatural power from a time when rebels defended their city from a traitor and his allies, rebels and privateers fought for liberty and supported the war movement in funding and provisions, naval agents conducted meetings, women defended their homesteads and nursed the sick, families hosted generals of importance, would-be spies taught as schoolmasters in local schools and both men and women gave their lives as martyrs for "the cause." Let the haunts of New London engulf you, as it is hard to find a city more entrenched in Connecticut's Revolutionary past than this.

EAST HADDAM

A LOYALIST'S PERSPECTIVE

DEVIL'S HOPYARD

There are abundant legends, myths and folklore stories that surround the 860 acres called Devil's Hopyard State Park. The name alone creates a sense of mystery and allure, a shadow of darkness. In fact, the exact history of how such a park acquired its name remains in debate, but the Connecticut Department of Energy and Environmental Protection (CT DEEP) has narrowed down the most well-known reasons for the naming of such a beautiful park surrounded with waterfalls, vista views, a gorgeous flowing river and peaceful quiet. CT DEEP acknowledged that fact and fiction have yet to be discerned from each other in the history of naming Devil's Hopyard.

One tale that indeed seems to have the broadest retelling and base in logic is this: There is a variety of potholes surrounding the Chapman Falls, the notorious cascading waterfall by the entrance to Devil's Hopyard. The potholes are remarkably cyclical in shape and come in all sizes, whether small (only inches) or large (several feet). They are wide, long and deep. Science dictates that these holes would be formed naturally as stones move downstream with the current and then subsequently become trapped in an eddy. When trapped, the stones would spin around, and a depression would wear into the rock on which it was trapped. As time passed, other stones would find themselves in the same rock area and expand the size of the pothole. Fascinating but not too mysterious.

This also would not have been common knowledge to anyone in the seventeenth century who was settling in the East Haddam area. Spiritual or supernatural causation was something they heavily believed in within Puritan New England.

So, what did these settlers surmise? It is theorized that they believed that the potholes were a sign that the devil passed by the falls. His tail got wet within the waterfalls, which angered him, so in a fury, he vandalized the rocks by burning holes into the stones with his hooves as he hastily bounded away. Now that is mysterious indeed. Why would the settlers believe the devil to be bounding about the hopyard in the first place? In such a small, serene natural area. Was there any other local legend to perpetuate supernatural occurrences in the area? We cannot say for certain, but it does indeed seem possible. As for the word *hopyard*, evidently there were many farmers in the area known for growing hops utilized in beer brewing. Perhaps that is where the name comes from, although that has not been confirmed of this particular land plot either.

However it may be, Devil's Hopyard is the name of this beautiful fishing, hiking and camping area set within rural East Haddam, and if you find yourself lucky enough to surround yourself in the nature of this area, you may indeed feel a little bit more or see an apparition. Many people with an interest in occult practice or paranormal happenings have congregated here as a sort of meeting place. Over the years, as this became a meeting ground, it may be that a ghostly portal of some kind has been opened. Many people believe that the devil himself can be found in the park sitting atop the bolder near the beginning of the sixty-foot falls, playing a fiddle while minions run about in the park around him.

Some people believe not only that the rocks are filled with little potholes where he walked but also that they form the shape of a cauldron or a devil's head—perpetuating the belief that the spirits are up to no good. Whether the devil ever played a part in the formation of Devil's Hopyard or considers it to be his playground is something that will always remain in local lore and encourage a certain amount of fascination. We may never know for sure if evil in the form of the devil stepped foot by Chapman Falls in Devil's Hopyard, but we do know of some evil occurrence that is embedded within the hopyard's memory.

There is a centuries-old history dating to the Revolution that may be responsible for at least one apparition sighted around the falls and the woods—something that doesn't seem to be the devil himself but still gives people a fright. It is an unarguable fact that there is something spiritual, something

Chapman Falls at Devil's Hopyard in East Haddam, near the foundation of the Beebe eighteenth-century gristmill, circa 2015.

historical and something that can only be described as supernatural around Devil's Hopyard State Park.

The Revolutionary War history surrounding Devil's Hopyard has only been fully revealed throughout the twenty-first century at the hands of a local man and history enthusiast, Louis Sorrentino. One evening in 2002,

Sorrentino had the strangest dream that he was living in another era—one before modern technology, before an immense world population, before America as we know it today was formed. Sorrentino felt that he was out of his own skin within the dream and had assumed the role of a local farmer or a miller. His surroundings looked familiar, somewhere he had been but couldn't place at the moment. Suddenly, the man he had become started getting beaten violently, pleading for help. Traumatic violence ensued, and then Sorrentino awoke.

The next day, Sorrentino was reflecting on his dream, on his own journeys of struggle and overcoming them, when he came to a realization. The place in his dream was one he had been to many times before: the Devil's Hopyard State Park and Chapman Falls. The next day, Sorrentino made his way there for a visit. It was a place he was familiar with, having grown up there frequenting the park as a child for walks, picnics and so on. This place and the not-so-far-away Gillette's Castle State Park make the perfect places for family. As he was strolling by Chapman Falls, with the dream he just had a not-so-distant memory, something caught his eye that seemed a bit out of place. It was a large piece of millstone sitting right in the Chapman Falls. It seemed fated that he found this, but at the moment, he was unsure why. What was this millstone's purpose? How did it get there? And how did he of all the thousands of people who come to the falls notice it? Sorrentino embarked on a fruitful journey that would take him into a Revolutionary-era past just like the one in his dream.

The *New York Times* reported that after he found it, "He called the municipal historian and checked out a historical marker near the stone. Both sources led him to the story of the Sons of Liberty toppling a stone into the falls to intimidate a Loyalist mill owner." Sorrentino was convinced that the millstone he spotted was this stone thrown violently down Chapman Falls by the Sons of Liberty in during their assault of Abner Beebe and destruction of his gristmill hundreds of years ago. A state archaeologist visited the site, and while unable to verify exactly how the stone arrived to the bottom of the falls, he was able to validate that it was found down the slope from the exact location of the foundation of the gristmill that had once been there in the eighteenth century. The foundation was in some places still present. Was it natural erosion, or was it thrown with a purpose? Sorrentino's research had only just begun.

A document provided by Mr. Sorrentino asserts that mills were key places of struggle due to their locations near natural resources—much like Chapman Falls. It was due to this importance that by 1777 or 1778 General

George Washington had "officially" ordered his officers to "remove the runnings stones from the mills so the enemy cannot easily recover them." This would prevent provisions from being given to local British forces. This took place in the early pre-Revolution and Revolutionary war years, when there were many rebels who were not assembled necessarily in military order but instead gathered in mobs devoted to their cause.

Abner Beebe was the mill owner near what is called Devil's Hopyard, and it is his mill foundation that still remains there today. Beebe was a prominent man, his family having been established in the East Haddam area for generations. He had an astute political mind and was a devoted Loyalist. He was highly educated, having graduated from Yale, and had the best intentions with his earnings, supporting a local poor person's burial site and also providing food for the less fortunate.

Beebe's Loyalist leanings were made clear and public. The earliest Bill of Rights established by the First Continental Congress was in 1774, and Beebe willingly made his disdain for and refusal to obey this new rebel regime clear. The era's *Connecticut Gazette*, now known as the *Hartford Courant*, quoted Dr. Abner Beebe as saying that he "refused to be tried by said Bill of Rights," and he believed that the "[British] government has a right to make whatever laws they please and it is our duty to obey." Abner and his uncle had even made public their opinion that British general Gage had a right to fire on people of Boston if they refused to surrender their weapons. The Beebes even said that it would be an act of treason for the people of Boston to oppose the new British-imposed taxes. Abner's brother, Asa, was another family Tory and lay leader in the Church of England and vocally pledged his allegiance to the British monarchy with his congregation at the beginning of every service. Additionally, his uncle served as a parish clerk in an openly British-supporting church of East Haddam.

The Beebes maintained prominent business transactions with one another and other Tories, consumed large amounts of British-import tea and made their unwavering support of the Loyalists and the monarchy abundantly clear. Abner Beebe's uncle was tortured by the Sons of Liberty. Early Sons of Liberty groups would sometimes torture those who spoke out against the cause for independence, and while they often acted on rogue missions, Governor Trumbull, George Washington and others ignored pleas for help from tortured Tories who became targets. Abner Beebe's published opinions on these matters, along with the fact that he was a mill owner, made him a prime target for the Sons of Liberty.

The violence done to the Beebe family included Abner's assault at Devil's Hopyard and the likely breaking of the millstone, detailed in Peter Oliver's account in 1781, which was written to justify England's violent response to the Revolutionary War in America. The account states:

> *A parish clerk of an Episcopal Church in East Haddam in Connecticut, a man of 70 years of age, was taken out of his bed in a cold night, and beat against his hearth by men who held him by his arms and legs. He was then laid across his horse, without his clothes, and drove to a considerable distance in that naked condition. His nephew, Dr. Abner Beebe, a physician complained of the bad usage of his uncle and spoke very freely in favor of the government; for which he was assaulted by a mob, stripped naked, and hot pitch was poured upon him, which blistered his skin. He was then carried to a hog sty and rubbed over with hog's dung. They threw the hog's dung in his face and rammed some of it down his throat and in that condition exposed to a company of women. His house was attacked, his windows broke, when some of his children were sick and a child of his went into distraction upon this treatment. His Gristmill was broke and persons prevented from grinding at it, and from having any connections with him. All these events occurred prior to the Battle of Lexington, when the rebels say the Rebellion began.*

Abner's assault took place on September 14, 1774. This horrid account was backed up in a letter dated that same day. The letter was a correspondence from Colonel Joseph Spencer to Governor Trumbull: "We learn that Dr. Beebe has been tarred and feathered on account of his Tory views and considers himself to be greatly abused."

No record has ever been found documenting whether Trumbull even replied. This was not uncommon to have lack of response from Governor Trumbull in such affairs. Although they could not officially sanction such horrendous behavior, especially prior to war being officially declared, the brutal treatment of Tories was unofficially condoned at the hands of the colonial leaders, and the Sons of Liberty were able to exercise great authority over the treatment of these Loyalists.

All of this and land records validate the history of the Beebe family and the attack of Dr. Abner Beebe at the hands of the Sons of Liberty. They also document the destruction of his gristmill, but what about throwing that stone down the millrace? More than one hundred years later, in 1881, a publication called the *Connecticut Valley Advertiser* had an article regarding the "large millstone" at Chapman Falls. The article states unequivocally that "Revolutionists broke open the mill and rolled the principal stone down the falls."

Now this does indeed match the account of Oliver's detailing that the gristmill was destroyed. Accounts of other gristmills being destroyed per Washington's order in 1777 and 1778 are written of in East Haddam, and documentation of seizures of gristmills is also presented. However, there is no statement regarding the old Beebe mill, as it was destroyed in 1774 and the stone lay broken, as thrown by the Tories down the falls. Sorrentino's research is filled with documentation of the stone's origins, the common practices in destroying gristmills in New England and the sometimes radical behavior of members of the Sons of Liberty—more than a decade of fact collecting continued by Lou and his associates. Because of this research, various historical societies and institutions have now been able validate not only the Beebe story but also that Chapman Falls in Devil's Hopyard is the site of the Beebe gristmill and the assault of Abner Beebe. They've been able to debunk false stories and lore that had the story twisted for years.

The truth of what happened is far more haunting than any folklore led locals to believe. Sorrentino's dreams and seemingly spiritual connection to Abner Beebe brought this entire story to the surface. Had Sorrentino not felt that kindred spirit and had Abner not reached out to Lou, the horrors and tale of that evening may have never been told again and may have been lost.

It has been conclusively determined that the broken Beebe millstone was thrown down the falls at the hands of the Sons of Liberty during their attack on Abner Beebe on September 14, 1774. After Sorrentino's news broke to various outlets around the country, the millstone became a tourist attraction of sorts, and it was agreed by the town and state that leaving it there would put it at risk of being stolen. The millstone was taken out of the falls by local groups in 2004 to preserve and protect it and was kept safely for a time by the East Haddam Historical Society. During these years, Sorrentino put together all the pieces of Beebe's horrendous ordeal and the life of a Tory against a rebellious population in eighteenth-century East Haddam. Even when Lou came face to face with local and state institutions filled with uncomfortable staff members, uncertain that they wanted to pursue a tale that painted any Son of Liberty in unfavorable light, Sorrentino continued in his pursuit. Beebe's story was as important as the rebels', even if it is an uncomfortable reality to acknowledge it. In fact, Lou was aware, as all true historians are, that history is written by the winners, but that doesn't

Broken millstone as thrown by Sons of Liberty and found at Devil's Hopyard, East Haddam, by Lou Sorrentino in 2002. *Courtesy of Lou Sorrentino.*

mean that there's not another side of the story that simply must be told. Sorrentino's path as a truth seeker paralleled troubles that Beebe would've felt but he endured—a message to never give up on what you believe.

If you want to get a look at this iconic artifact of New England history, never fear. This remarkable item will be on display by the summer of 2017 at the Smithsonian National Museum of American History in Washington, D.C. Sorrentino's persistence and research did not go unnoted by the nation's most respected institution of historical artifacts. This was an amazing accomplishment for Sorrentino and for the legacy of Abner Beebe's family. Lou continues to feel the haunts but only in a comforting sense. Getting to know the spirit of Beebe has served as continuous inspiration in his daily work of helping those liberate themselves from the disease of addiction and has even translated into songs he has written. He spreads the story of what liberty means, as well as the importance of making sure that every generation does not trod on another's rights in pursuit of its own.

Apparitions are frequently seen around the falls of a man in colonial-era clothing looking downtrodden and old, asking for help. He is seen around the falls and sometimes in the woods. In addition, whether people are empathic or the spirit of Beebe has tried to call out to them, people find themselves feeling pushed around and falling down around the falls when they had felt otherwise balanced. Perhaps they are picking up on the energies of Beebe's past. Camera batteries die along the hiking trails, only to come back to life when people depart, and others wander the small wooded area, following the tread on path, only to get turned around and lost, walking an area they were certain they had already passed. They wonder if something, the ghost or even the devil, is changing the woods around them, making them feel like they can't escape. Whether you are there for the fishing, hiking or a romantic picnic, you may hear whispers in the wind and see movement out of the corner of your eye. If you calmly turn toward the movement, you may be expecting to see another hiker strolling by but instead find that you are standing next to the ghosts of Devil's Hopyard, possibly even the tortured Abner Beebe himself.

Whether the Sons of Liberty considered the motivation of such a vicious attack to be pure in their pursuit of independence or whether it was merely an unwarranted attack of violence, it is undisputed fact that this night forever changed Abner Beebe, his family and the property now known as Devil's Hopyard. What happened to Dr. Abner Beebe on that fateful September night was nothing short of brutal. How can an event of such torture not leave an impact on the property? For Abner Beebe, on September 14, 1774, the devil may have indeed walked through the area of Chapman Falls in East Haddam. It forever changed the life and landscape that he had always known, leaving behind only a haunting presence surrounding the entirety of Devil's Hopyard State Park.

A COLLECTION OF CONNECTICUT'S REVOLUTIONARY SITES

Connecticut Revolutionary sites are abundant—some with reported spirit activity and some without. A Revolutionary past haunts the state whether with the traditional wandering ghost or a history that continues to thrive.

BOOK BARN, NIANTIC/EAST LYME

More than twenty-five Revolutionary War soldiers are believed to be buried within the town limits of East Lyme, including Niantic. Once on a popular route for travel and taverns, men would have found themselves passing through here on eighteenth-century journeys via horse or foot. The Book Barn is known to have numerous accounts of ghostly activity and was investigated in April 2015 by DKS Paranormal and Seaside Shadows. Accounts and investigative evidence showed proof of a child spirit, matronly spirits helping with property upkeep, a young man who may have suffered in a nearby car accident and even some EVPs suggesting that men from the eighteenth century wandered through the property. The most unique bookseller in New England has numerous houses throughout the property, and for book lovers, it's a fantasy world filled with friendly proprietors, coves, sheds, barns and buildings filled with books of every kind, as well as a few friendly cats that will help you pick something unique out. A must-see for books and haunts in Connecticut.

HUNTINGTON HOMESTEAD MUSEUM, SCOTLAND

The birthplace of Declaration of Independence signer and Continental Congress president Samuel Huntington, this unique property sits on its original eighteenth-century foundation. Stone walls, abandoned roads and the mysterious allure of an era long since passed abound on the historic property. It is a favorite of local investigative teams to investigate, members of which insist that sights and frights abound within the museum's wall.

Portrait of Samuel Huntington as painted by Charles Wilson Peale in 1783. *Courtesy of Wikipedia.*

GRISWOLD INN AND RESTAURANT, ESSEX

Established in 1776, the Griswold Inn is one of the oldest operating taverns and inns in the country. Essex's shoreline was a main highway for merchants and soldiers and in the War of 1812. The Griswold Inn was taken over by the British, who used it as their site of operations during the war. Some regard the War of 1812 as the true "War for Independence," as it wasn't until after this that Americans were out of British control once and for all. The British raid on Essex and burning of ships in the War of 1812 are a major part of history today. Prior to this, though, it is believed that Patriots and Tories alike frequented the Griswold Inn and tavern for a local beverage. Employees and guests alike have seen the apparition of a man in a tricorn hat and period attire in the tavern room and the kitchen and perhaps even strolling the dining room. A place of history and romance in aesthetically beautiful Essex, the Griswold Inn is also a place of reported eighteenth-century ghosts.

Webb-Deane-Stevens Museum, Wethersfield

A collection of four historic houses—Joseph Webb House, Silas Deane House, Isaac Stevens House and Buttolph-Williams House—this museum boasts one of the largest historical experiences in Connecticut, a revival of eighteenth- and nineteenth-century lifestyles in New England. The Webb House, built in 1752, was where George Washington continued plans for the Battle at Yorktown alongside Rochambeau. This was the duo's headquarters for planning in May 1781. The Silas Deane House was home to Deane and his family; Deane was secretary of Connecticut's Committee of Correspondence and delegate to the Continental Congress in 1774. A close friend of founding fathers, Deane was often working with Benjamin Franklin, and he and his wife, Elizabeth, hosted both John Adams and George Washington at their home in the 1770s. Due to gossip and miscommunication, Deane's distinguished reputation was later brought into question. The other two houses were built in the eighteenth century—the Buttolph-Williams House in 1711 (it stood during the Revolution) and the Stevens House not until the latter part of the century. Four historic buildings filled with activity and visitors—it's no surprise that many who walk the halls feel the sense of eyes on them as they walk through.

Keeler Tavern, Ridgefield

Cannonball lodged in the side of Keeler Tavern during the Battle at Ridgefield in 1777. *Courtesy of Wikipedia.*

The Battle of Ridgefield on April 27, 1777, is said to be the event that rallied the support of Patriots throughout America, further dedicating their involvement to the rebel cause and the Continental army. Their loss to the British angered locals. General Tryon and his British force, under command of the royal governor of New York province, landed on western Connecticut shores, where they marched to Danbury, destroyed Continental army supplies and provisions and fought off a small number of defenders. Connecticut militia leaders immediately received word of their presence, including Benedict Arnold (then on the American

Map of the Battle at Ridgefield as drawn in 1780. *Courtesy of Wikipedia.*

side), Benjamin Silliman and David Wooster. They gathered in the Keeler Tavern basement as a headquarters and instructed seven hundred men in how to fight off the British, who were approaching through Ridgefield. A barricade was set on North Main Street, and fighting ensued. A cannonball was launched at the Keeler Tavern by the British, and that cannonball remains in the walls of the Keeler Tavern to this day as a commemoration of that fateful day and impactful battle. With such intensity having taken place in and around the tavern, many believe that it has a residual haunting—you can go within and almost relive the battle and the Revolutionary air the building once had.

Putnam Memorial State Park, Redding

The now state park was the site of a winter war encampment for Revolutionary soldiers serving under Major General Israel Putnam during the winter of 1778–79. More than three thousand Revolutionary soldiers were housed in camps throughout Redding in order to keep a protective eye on the once-attacked Danbury and storage facilities that they had since replenished and were vital to Continental army troops. Remains of the encampment exist on the property today, and any soldiers who did not survive the winter are believed to be buried on-site. Legend has it that one of the soldiers returned to his previous encampment and lived among rocks in a type of cave, now called Philip's Cave in his honor. Tired of the local thief living in the abandoned encampment, a local farmer shot him dead. Some believe that Philip still haunts the Putnam Memorial Park, a place he longed to return to and where he was subsequently killed. Locals who attend the park for picnics or for a stroll have reported rapid light movements around them even as the sun sets, or while driving by at night, they notice the distinct movement of orbs surrounding the area.

BIBLIOGRAPHY

BOOKS

Baker, Mark Allen. *Connecticut Families of the Revolution: American Forebears from Burr to Wolcott*. Charleston, SC: The History Press, 2014.

———. *Spies of Revolutionary Connecticut: From Benedict Arnold to Nathan Hale*. Charleston, SC: The History Press, 2014.

Child, Frank S. *Being an Account of the Thaddeus Burr Homestead: Fairfield, Connecticut, 1654–1915*. N.p, 1915.

Ellet, Elizabeth Fries. *The Queens of American Society*. Philadelphia, PA: Porter & Coates, 1873.

Lee, William D. *The Sun Tavern and the Red Admiral*. Agawam, MA: Damianos Publishing, 2013.

Lehman, Eric D. *Homegrown Terror: Benedict Arnold and the Burning of New London*. Middletown, CT: Wesleyan University Press, 2014.

Oliver, Peter. "Peter Oliver's Origin and Progress of the American Rebellion." N.p., 1781.

Society of the Founders of Norwich, Connecticut. *A Report on Leffingwell Inn, Norwichtown, Connecticut*. Norwich, CT: Society of the Founders of Norwich, 1957.

ARTICLES

Altimari, Dave. "Lebanon 'War Office' Played Central Role in Revolutionary War Planning." *Hartford Courant*, May 23, 2014.

Bendici, Ray. "Devil's Hopyard, East Haddam." *Damned Connecticut*, March 2009.

Benson, Adam. "Leffingwell House to Showcase Its Arnold Artifacts." *Norwich Bulletin*, September 19, 2013.

Bowles, Adam. "Uncovering a Millstone Who-Done-It." *New York Times*, January 25, 2004.

Brophy, Andrew. "Burning of Fairfield to Be Remembered on Wednesday." *Fairfield Patch*, July 4, 2010.

Clark, Marlene. "A Lot of Digging, in the Records, Exposes Millstone Myth." *Hartford Courant*, April 7, 2004.

Connecticut Department of Energy & Environmental Protection. "Fort Griswold Battlefield State Park." 2015.

Connecticut Gazette. Various untitled articles, 1774–76.

Connecticut Valley Advertiser. Untitled article, July 16, 1881.

Fairfield Museum and History Center. "House that Witnessed History." 2015.

———. "Sun Tavern: Did George Washington Sleep Here?" 2015.

Fitzpatrick, Beth Cooney. "Fairfield Famous: Thaddeus and Eunice Burr." *Fairfield Living*, 2014.

Fleischman, John. "Devil's Advocate." *New London (CT) Day*, December 28, 1999.

Hopper, Jessica. "Voices from 230 Years Ago Still Heard on Groton Bank." *New London (CT) Day*, October 29, 2014.

Kimball, Carol. "Anna Warner Bailey, Our Petticoat Heroine: The Groton Story." Anna Warner Bailey Chapter, National Society Daughters of the American Revolution. AnnaWarnerBaileyDAR.org.

O'Connell, Michael. "$158.4 M Facelift Gives American History Museum New Outlook." *Federal News Radio*, September 16, 2014.

Rogers, Ernest E. "The Joshua Hempstead Diary." *New London Gazette*, July 6, 1901.

Sorrentino, Lou. "Historical Importance of Beebe's Mills at Devil's Hopyard." Private document, 2007.

———. "Meaning of Freedom." Private document, 2013.

St. Louis Post-Dispatch. "Stephen Hempstead." April 25, 2014.

ELECTRONIC SOURCES

The Burr History and Genealogy Site. "The Family Burr History." http://www.burrcook.com/history/burrhisc.htm.

Connecticut Department of Energy & Environmental Protection. "Devil's Hopyard State Park, East Haddam." http://www.ct.gov/deep/cwp/view.asp?a=2716&q=325188.

Connecticut History on the Web. "British Burn Fairfield—Today in History: July 7." http://connecticuthistory.org/british-burn-fairfield.

———. "Christopher Leffingwell Born—Today in History: June 11." http://connecticuthistory.org/statesman-and-businessman-christopher-leffingwell-born-today-in-history.

———. "The Joshua Hempstead Diary: A Window into Colonial Connecticut." http://connecticuthistory.org/joshua-hempstead-diary-a-window-into-colonial-connecticut.

Connecticut Landmarks. "Hempsted Houses." http://www.ctlandmarks.org//content/hempsted-houses.

Connecticut Society of Sons of the American Revolution. "Trumbull War Office." http://www.ctsar.org/sites/le-waroffice.htm.

Dartmouth Collections. "Shaw, Nathaniel Junior." https://collections.dartmouth.edu/occom/html/ctx/personoography/pers0479.ocp.html.

The Forgotten Founders. "Norwich Revolutionary War." http://theforgottenfounders.com/tag/norwich-revolutionary-war.

Governor Trumbull House DAR. "Welcome to the Governor Jonathan Trumbull House and Wadsworth Stable." http://govtrumbullhousedar.org/index.html.

Historic Structures. "Leffingwell Inn, Norwich, Connecticut." http://www.historic-structures.com/ct/norwich/leffingwell_inn.php.

The Massachusetts Society Sons of the American Revolution, Founded 1889. "Mob Attacks on Loyalists in Massachusetts 1774." http://www.massar.org/mob-attacks-on-loyalists-in-massachusetts-august-1774.

Revolutionary Connecticut. "Devil's Hopyard Millstone." http://www.revolutionaryct.com/devils-hopyard-millstone.

———. "Fairfield County: Sun Tavern, Burr Mansion." http://www.revolutionaryct.com/tag/fairfield-county.

Town of Fairfield, Connecticut. "The Burning of Fairfield during the American Revolution." http://www.fairfieldct.org/content/10724/12146/12165.aspx.

Wikipedia. "Benedict Arnold." https://en.wikipedia.org/wiki/Benedict_Arnold.

———. "Lauzun's Legion." https://en.wikipedia.org/wiki/Lauzun%27s_Legion.

———. "Talk: Nathaniel Shaw." https://en.wikipedia.org/wiki/Talk:Nathaniel_Shaw.

PRIMARY SOURCES

Leffingwell, Christopher. "Christopher Leffingwell to George Washington, July 15, 1789." Letter. From Founders Online, George Washington Papers. http://founders.archives.gov/documents/Washington/05-03-02-0111.

———. "Christopher Leffingwell to John Hancock, Referred to Wythe & Committee, November 29, 1775." Letter. From William & Mary Law Library. Wythepedia. http://lawlibrary.wm.edu/wythepedia/index.php/Christopher_Leffingwell_to_John_Hancock,_referred_to_Wythe_%26_Committee,_29_November_1775.

Palfrey, William. Series 5 Financial Papers. Vouchers and Receipt Accounts. From Library of Congress, George Washington Papers, 1741–99. http://memory.loc.gov/cgi-bin/ampage?collId=mgw5&fileName=gwpage024.db&recNum=116.

Spencer, Joseph. "Joseph Spencer to Governor Trumbull, September 14, 1774." Letter. From American Archives.

INTERVIEWS

Andriopoulos, Evan. Personal interview by author. E-mail, August 28, 2015.

Colley, Brent. Personal interview by author. Telephone, August 27, 2015.

Correll, Kayla and Steve Manuel. Personal interview by author. New London, Connecticut, March 19, 2015.

D'Agostino, Thomas. Personal interview by author. Putnam, March 22, 2015.

Davis, Marilyn. Personal interview by author. Telephone, March 22, 2015.

Denniston, Shamus. Personal interview by author. Telephone, March 17, 2015.

Emerson, Jennifer. Personal interview by author. Telephone, August 12, 2015.

Farlow, Camilla. Personal interview by author. Norwich, Connecticut, March 16, 2015.

Flegert, Matthew. Personal interview by author. Coventry, Connecticut, July 27, 2015.

Guidebeck, Richard. Personal interview by author. Norwich, Connecticut, March 16, 2015.

Knapp, Kurt. Personal interview by author. Telephone, June 3, 2015.

Lee, William D. Personal interview by author. Trumbull, March 26, 2015.

Marshall, Stephen. Personal interview by author. Lebanon, Connecticut, March 12, 2015.

Matsumoto, Carol. Personal interview by author. Preston, Connecticut, March 11, 2015.

Nagy, Barbara. Personal interview by author. New London, Connecticut, May 19, 2015.

Onofrio, Dominick and Dan Leroy. Personal interview by author. E-mail, July 31, 2015.

Packard, Dave. Personal interview by author. East Haddam and Lebanon, Connecticut, April 30, 2015.

Pagliuco, Linda. Personal interview by author. Coventry, Connecticut, March 20, 2015.

Reis, Carlos. Personal interview by author. Fishkill, New York. June 27, 2015.

Shaw, Stephen. Personal interview by author. Lebanon, Connecticut, March 12, 2015.

Sorrentino, Lou. Personal interview by author. Telephone, January 6, 2016.

About the Author

Courtney McInvale is a Connecticut native and descendant of numerous Revolutionary War Patriots. She was born and raised in a real-life haunted house in East Hampton. In fact, her childhood home was investigated by the Warren family during her teenage years. Since then, she has always been attracted to the paranormal and has learned of her unique abilities as a spirit medium and put them into practice. Courtney also developed a love and passion for the study of history and a dedication to the importance of blending both historical and paranormal research for accurate assertions. Ms. McInvale is a graduate of Catholic University of America with a degree in international politics. After varying government jobs, Courtney migrated back to Connecticut, where she established Seaside Shadows Haunted History Tours in Mystic Country, Connecticut, and that is where she began writing paranormal history books. McInvale is the author of *Haunted Mystic*, published by The History Press in 2014. Courtney resides in eastern Connecticut with her loving husband, Marty. When Courtney and Marty aren't chasing ghosts of New England's colorful past, they can be found spending time with their furry friends: Danny Boy, Lennon and Lovebug.